# EMBODIMENT
*and other poems*

## Books by Arthur Gregor

*Poems*

Embodiment (1982)
The Past Now (1975)
Selected Poems (1971)
A Bed by the Sea (1970)
Figure in the Door (1968)
Basic Movements (1966)
Declensions of a Refrain (1957)
Octavian Shooting Targets (1954)

*For Children*

The Little Elephant *Photos by Ylla* (1956)
1 2 3 4 5, Verses *Photos by Robert Doisneau* (1956)
Animal Babies *Photos by Ylla* (1959)

## Plays

Fire! (The Illini Theatre Guild, University of Illinois, Urbana)
    1952
Continued Departure (The Cubiculo Theatre, New York) 1968,
    1970 (in *Accent*, summer issue, 1951)
The Door Is Open (The Cubiculo Theatre, New York) 1970

# EMBODIMENT
*and other poems*

## Arthur Gregor

The Sheep Meadow Press
New York

*Cover Drawing by Jose Ribera.*
*Photo by Richard Moss.*

**Library of Congress Cataloging in Publication Data**

Gregor, Arthur, 1923-
    Embodiment, and other poems.

    Includes bibliographical references.
    I. Title.
PS3557.R434E4          811'.54          82-3268
ISBN 0-935296-28-X                      AACR2
ISBN 0-935296-29-8 (pbk.)

**ACKNOWLEDGMENTS**

Grateful acknowledgment is made to the editors of the following
magazines in which many of the new poems were first published, for
their permission to reprint them here. Slight revisions have been made
in a good many of them.

HUDSON REVIEW: "Songs of Belonging" — *The Rising; To be Part of; The
Loire at St. Firmin; Hanna's House; At St. Benoit; At Sancere; At
Chartres; In the Town of Chartres; Quai Voltaire; My Soul, A Girl,*
SOUTHERN REWIEW: *The Power of Art, The Pine,* SEWANEE REVIEW; *Val
de Loire, Contours,* MICHIGAN QUARTERLY REVIEW: *To Emily, Abun-
dance, Now,* PEMBROKE MAGAZINE: *The Ravages, Unmolested,* NEW
LETTERS: *At the Trough,* CUMBERLAND POETRY REVIEW: *Clear Thoughts,
His Departure,* NIAGARA MAGAZINE: *Two Poems in Memory of Jean
Garrigue*—One, Two, MARILYN: *On The Long Island Railroad* (under
the title *Reflection*), POETRY NOW: *A Visit, As Though in Pale Morning,
The Shaper of Words on His Instruction,* HARPER'S MAGAZINE: *The Link,*
THE NATION: *Crowd of Absences, The Healing, Two-Sided, Markings,*
PEARL (Denmark) *Muse* (under the title *Unnamed*), The Kiss; Cul-de-Sac
appeared originally in THE NEW YORKER; MUDFISH: *The Rescue*

    Stanley Moss read this manuscript with an accuracy, empathy and
intuitive intelligence rarely encountered; I wish to thank him for this
and for his many helpful suggestions.

The thirty-five poems selected for this volume in chronological order appeared first in the following magazines and books:

Blackout appeared in POETRY, Octavian Shooting Targets, 1954 (hereafter cited as OST), Selected Poems, 1971 (hereafter cited as SP); The Chase in THE CRYSTAL CABINET, DECLENSIONS OF A REFRAIN, 1957, SP; Basic Movements in POETRY, Basic Movements, 1966 (hereafter cited as BM); At Twenty or So in POETRY, BM, SP; Spirits Dancing in THE NEW YORKER, BM, SP; A Single Flower of the Field in VOICES, BM, SP; Assisi and Environs in SEWANEE REVIEW, BM, SP; A Sunbather in Late October and Runaway Spirit in BM, SP; The Likeness in THE NEW YORKER, Figure in the Door, 1968 (hereafter cited as FITD), SP; The Calm in THE NEW YORKER, FITD, SP; Reply to a Friend in New England in THE NEW YORKER, FITD, SP; Shadowplay in THE NEW YORKER, FITD, SP; Don Carlos, Saturday Afternoon in THE NATION, FITD, SP; Exiled in THE NATION, FITD, SP; First Snow, Brooklyn Harbor in SEWANEE REVIEW, FITD, SP; Late Last Night in THE NATION, FITD, SP; Irreconcilables in THE NEW YORKER, FITD, SP; Gentle Lamb in THE NEW YORKER, FITD, SP; The Unworldliness That He Creates in POETRY, FITD, SP; Unalterables in THE NEW YORKER; A Bed by the Sea, 1970 (hereafter cited as ABBTS), SP; The Statue in POETRY, ABBTS, SP; A Soldier Waiting His Turn in a Barber Shop in SP; Two on the Firebird in POETRY, SP; History in COMMON-WEAL, SP; Old Coat in NEW YORK POETRY, SP; The Tenuous Line in SP; The Look Back in THE NEW YORKER, The Past Now, 1975 (hereafter cited as TPN); Les Nuits d'Été in MILL MOUNTAIN REVIEW, TPN; Process of Recapturing in TPN; On Behalf of Orpheus in HELLCOAL ANNUAL, TPN; Wind to Human Voice in HARPERS MAGAZINE, TPN; Wilderness Child in THE NEW YORKER, TPN; Like Laocoön in THE NATION, TPN. The years of publication and the publishers of the books were: Octavian Shooting Targets, Dodd, Mead & Co., 1954; Declensions of a Refrain, Poetry London-New York Books, Dodd, Mead, 1957; Basic Movements, The Gyre Press, 1966; Figure in the Door, Doubleday & Co., 1968; A Bed by the Sea, Doubleday & Co., 1970; Selected Poems, Doubleday & Co., 1971; The Past Now, Doubleday & Co., 1975.

Distributed by Persea Books
225 Lafayette St.
New York, N.Y. 10012

Printed in the United States of America

# Contents

# THIRTY-FIVE SELECTED POEMS, 1947-1974

*It is not to be seen in the appearances*
*That tell of it.*
— Wallace Stevens

*I am the light of consciousness in all thoughts and*
*perceptions, and the light of love in all feelings.*
— Sri Atmananda

# First Snow, Brooklyn Harbor

1.

Driven by a music of which their every move
in a mood of love, the loftier side of them
in dreams, are parts; unconsciously out for a sign
that is a gesture of the song they do not hear:
who among those who stopped along the promenade
facing the waterfront could have regarded
the first flake of the first snow this season
as nothing but the substance that he is?

Unless someone had ventured out, had left
the customary ways of recognizing form
and light and shade; unless someone endowed
with a rare inner quality had looked
and found the single substance holding forms
flowing from his eyes and breaking from
the heart where it lies and not unlike
calm waters beneath frozen mountains, waits
beneath all icy grounds where light like
sound in the unsaid aspect in each song
glistens beyond sight;

                    unless someone had pierced
the surfaces and stood entirely immersed
within the substance of all forms, within
the very center of all thoughts and shapes
that like the very breath of time rise from
the one sure thing toward which all strive;
unless someone in such state had given
existence to the first flake falling and from
beyond the range of sight proclaimed the whiteness
that streaked across the eye in streams
and in a time too imminent to calculate
dissolved, absolved the heaviness of the world:

who among the solitary men looking out
beyond the river and the ocean piers
into a changed and changing distance, could
have known that these are closely linked:
the forms across the waterway, the lights
barely discernible that alternate, the snow
that falls, the physical significance of snow,
the revival in the hearts of solitary men
of dreams?

How could they have known that these
are more than linked, are one with that
which glistens in and between the flakes,
are the same as what the fall of snow implies?

And what it evokes in them, how could they know
it is the same as what they—solitary men,
distances apart, gazing beyond the river,
ocean-landing where they stand—in this
first snow are looking toward, are looking at?

2.

The thing itself that lives, the dominance
of that which is so close to all it is
the heart of all; in which the first sign
originates and descends into sight as snow,
whose nature is unfathomable although
in this and every scene implied by some
incomprehensible means like a music
that cannot be heard: O what they do not know
is that the distances expand within them:
what they are looking toward is where they are.

They do not know departure is the pain they carry;
that circumstance has forced on them a burden
the removal of which is the change they seek
in dreams of a journey and the joy they sense
of what it must be like the instant of arrival.

In a fall of snow, the first of the season,
they stand and dream and watch the footprints
disappear in the will of heaven; absorb the sounds
of water-objects drown in a deeper music,
and shiver as light breaks in their hearts
and something vastly woeful hangs at their eyes.

For, if these men are in no way exceptional,
if they are not endowed with a sacred privilege
to look and find the answer contained in the question,
fire in the ultimate regions of cold, arrival
in the act of departing, the indivisible total
in each divided vanishing footfall
as each flake contains all of the snow.
If it is not for them to set forth
provoking customary habits with
a selfless motive for daring and a song
to rely on from loss to finding, they cannot know this,
though they do surely sense how enormous are
the heights that exist within the pattern of Being:

Beyond their conditioned manner of reaching, near them,
with no more than a turn of their shoulder,
they can glimpse the regions of high-minded men:
the heart which is wisdom, the pleasure, the welcome,
the compassionate quality in music.
The burden circumstance has forced on them
is a condition abolished by a shift within them,
as the heaviness of the world is abolished by
a sudden decision which is the first snow
of the season.

*     *     *

            And if they cannot know themselves
possessors of the single substance
of which all of the harbor before them,
and the forms that make up the harbor
and the transformation of everything in
and around them which they attribute to snow,
are made of;

and if they cannot assume the stand
that that which is in them, into which
each flake dissolves and all perceptions flow,
is changeless, and they the beholder of changes; —

they do, just the same, sense with longing
something of permanence, knowing, as they do,
only the changes; and for a moment absorbed
in a depth that is the quiet of the whiteness
descending, question:

what are they caught in?
Where does it come from, the dream, the thoughts
of which they are conscious? Has the snow
brought back the ways they knew as children,
dreams that have caused them embarrassment in gesture,
quick glances?

And if they cannot recognize
themselves in the radiance of unreal faces
like spirits in a net of snow; and if
what they know is not the supreme conquest
by achievement but the mystery like a sob
within them, they do, just the same, sense it:
the nearness that is far:

ranges of oceans,
distance and music in the sounds of water-objects;
and grieve for the breath of an angel they feel
in the footfall they cling to for an all-engrossing,
all-encompassing vastly beautiful moment
before the outlines that attest to the fact
that a human has been there, turn into snow.

*1960*

# NEW POEMS

*1975-1980*

*One*

## The Link

# The Link

1.

Picture Ariadne outside the mud labyrinth
at its exit in the sunlight
bright as sand
throwing a blossom-strung thread
white streamer
into its depth
to light up
the beloved's path...

2.

Can you think of a more courageous act
than to face backward
and cast the best you have
best you can give
into a depth
you cannot be sure of
toward a source
you cannot see?

## Cul-De-Sac

Here in the public garden
among others lingering—
lingering musically in the dark of
trees, the statues' thoughtful poses—
here in the once royal park
as you look toward the daylight
dense and dying beyond the streets

you are tempted. To wipe from you
this life that is insufficient.
To turn. To have but one
concern: the music

to be taken back
as though by someone's hand
who knows exactly where you want to reach

to return
to the gravel path's end
(or is it the beginning?)
where the park's great
wrought iron gates open
to the deep glow
of the dying light
to the music's source
the shadowed classic lawn
to your own dark shape
coming close.

# To Emily

When I found myself faced directly,
eyes searching out mine
as if for fresh sightings or contest,
lips whose pensive stillness
changed before me to fullness
as if turned to flesh on canvas
—an old, a not forgotten land
floats close, a deeply remembered tune
from a ship out of the distance—
and then almost audibly
from the barely parted lips
the words: *yes, yes...*

When I faced this in that face
I thought of you, Emily,
at the top of your stairs
all in white, a white branch
of greeting in your hand,
your impossible heart
bursting into tiny, gold-blue,
twittering, fluttering birds,—

thought of you and understood
why you could not take
that first step down,
understood, when I looked into
the eyes before me, at the lips
so eloquent by now,
how you were torn,
why even then you would have
preferred to turn
and not descend to
the dark figure awaited
and pacing below.

# The Healing

In the shimmering moment
when dream is left behind
like a glistening sea
looked back on quickly,
in the shimmering moment
that at rare times
enters awareness just as
day's bulk dawns:

without form or guise
pure presence that
is always only yours.
As once long ago
when I looked up from the sickbed
and you sat at its edge
in the light that streamed in
through the gauze as I woke.

# On the Long Island Railroad

Winter trees

behind them
houses at quick
intervals

the silver of winter trees
houses behind them
disappearing speedily
as the train flies past

the sparkle
of sun behind trees
of light around
silvery branches and stems

a sparkle of light
seen from
the window of a rapid train

a glittering as of
sun on the sea

and I am again made to know
that something else persists

something unseen continues

What I must hold on to
must hold on to:
who has ever held it?

# Opposite

A shy outgoingness,
gladness and surprise
in a look I saw on a crowded bus
were clear indication to me
that sameness had been beheld.
Although I could not tell
at whom the look was directed,
I knew one face had met another
as if coming upon itself in
trembling water—amid reflected
tall grass, pine trees, and flowers
afloat; had seen a face there
that when gazed on for a time
is recognized not as one's own
but in whom one's own has lain
deep in its wateriness, beneath
the leaf-filled surface, a shine
recaptured, its features
always known: the face
more familiar than one's own.

# Contours

Everything I try to hold on to
and think for a while I do —
the stranger I pass
but cross with into love
in my mind, bright body-contours
I pull with me from dream into the day,
some face reflecting what
I also am, and mine
its mirror in return —

dissolved the instant that
it streams to eye, to hand,
dissociated though remembered —
settles elsewhere than in
the memory it crowds and strains;
among unimagined colorings
in a space incomprehensible
and beyond the painful paling.

# Markings

You have not asked to be where you are.
The sunset cloud-bouquet is spectacular.
A schooner in a dream. You know by now
that forms, events you desire
can come to little more than this.

Tints, clouds that will not make
an absence; a betrothed, a friend
descending from a ship as if
the arrival of someone you loved
were a photograph in your hand!

Just once, as if the approaching craft
were forever nearing,
the wind-blown figure
forward near the prow, just once
to love, to live as if
flower skies never change...

But you have absorbed by now the limits,
the markings deep within you.
The constant vanishings you have
are not the permanence you crave.

# Two-sided

What I love the most
is not attached,
a cloudlike shape
I think of as wandering
across some sea,
a wind-and-light fabric
between a water surface and
low branches of a tree,
someone's whistling
so far out in the dark
you can just make out
the shadow leaping
dangerously
on the far edge of a dock.

Yet here is a paradox:
without contact made
and more than that
without at least
modest attachment
what I love the most—
the stir in the thing
that moves with grace,
fiercely independent—
does not leap in the dark
does not go whistling
in and out of sight
unpredictably
on precipitous ledges of the night.

# The Ravages

Though he had not yet walked
among settings once ideal
but now marred by ravages,
cypress lanes that lead
to many views past many ruins,
broken steps to
cities of classic gods, —

though he had not yet suffered
a change from sights that excite
to letdown, a look
faltering and grey,
he looked at me as if he had
(he was at most fifteen);
so young, so soon so sad.

Why at me? Could he sense
that I too
had grasped entirely
what lay ahead of me
when I was fifteen:
perfection held—and by it held—
in a stormy flash,

instants of love
carried aloft, joy,
a blaze of sun on stones
dissolved in air,
to nothing in darkening streets,
remembered and remembering shapes
crowding an endless interior...?

Could he sense when he looked at me
how well I knew
what he would have to come to know:
the descent,
love's aftermath he too,
so young, so soon so sad,
will not prevent?

# The Rescue

We must have known each other
in a time, a life we cannot remember,
struggling from going under,
to discern the sun in a murderous storm,
must have formed a closeness then

no matter what the precise
circumstance when
struggling to rescue the body
the body within the body
that cries out to be salvaged
to be lifted from the rage of mists
into shadowed spaces of the sun.

Some such engagement must have been
ours, ours together
or I would not have felt drawn
to try to rescue with you now
that part in each of us
always in need of rescue.

As I cannot recall we had met
we must have been together then,
then or even before the time
before the crash no one remembers.

# The Kiss

Now, afterward,
after the affection that rose from us both
had held us as if it too were a physical body,

now it is not the man in me
that has stepped out
strengthened into
the space the embrace has cleared
the shine of heaven

not the man, nor the youth in me
that has stepped forth like
a statue with muscular legs
into the admiring circle of crowds
that have come from far

not that, nor the girl in me
drawn forth as if summoned
and trembling behind scarfs:

not these, but the child in me
unchanged and unchanging—
the child that has come out, come forth
as if lifted up
by arms out of clouds.

## Unmolested

We had forgotten
there is a bloom, white and fresh,
delicate spray always in season
we had known once how to reach

had known how to keep the dark apart
to glimpse the bloom
and taste the scent
demanded by the heart.

Had known then, for how else
could it now be remembered,
could it now be sensed again
when — intuitively, accidentally? —

at your touch on my shoulder
and mine on your chest, we stumbled, barefoot, on
the unmolested green
where the white blossom grows?

# A Visit

You are there
remain behind at the boundary of sleep
and I can look back at you
as I am drawn away and you recede
like a white mountain from
the back of a car.

And you grow smaller, smaller
will soon be lost behind
a road, behind the actions and
appointments that make up
the hours of the day.

But you are there, there are
indications that you are
like the long, wet line in the sand,
dense trees and blossoms on the ground,
or the smile on someone asleep

that tell of
a sea that has been there,
of a season that has passed,
of a visit
that is taking place.

# At the Trough

Weary of the day, of small-
mindedness and petty maneuverings,
I drove out toward the hills
and stopped near the fields
where sheep and cattle graze.
Hearing the birds from all sides
and seeing such animals, trees,

and hills in hazy distances
I soon felt refreshed, especially
as I watched the sheep marching
to drink at the trough outside
the shed. What do they know —
I thought as they stood there
drinking — what do they know

when later in their sleep
they do not dream; where are
they then? Where I am when I,
having left the day, lie deeper than
in dream, and drink; — neither they
nor I aware of the body then,
but drink, drink, till I wake?

What comfort as I drove off
to think that when in the dark
inside their shed they sleep
drenched in an innocence
they at least need never leave,
and when I have gone to sleep
I am no different then,
no different then from them.

# Clear Thoughts

I wake up with a start.
Clear thoughts have taken hold.
*Thoughts* is not the right word.
Rather it is that a fixed condition
announces itself, like winds
holding the crowns of trees.
The child you are is your truth.
It has been behind the words
formed into lines on the page,
behind your reaching toward
another in the dark, behind
your lying stretched out,
your forehead touching the ground
at the top of stairs, waters
roaring below, above you
faces hidden by clouds.

Clarification continues like an
incomprehensible unfolding in what
turns out to be a dream,
there are acts, a few, a few
—and lying there was one of them—
that occur outside of time,
are repeated now, now in the dark:
the cryptic cry, the sky breaking open
above gnarled trees and crosses on the hill,
the genius of geniuses perceiving as
harmonious, incredible sounds
the tensions between heaven and hell
—things that do not connect,
no satisfaction to the mind
to wake with a start in the night
to a clarity surpassing stars.

# Two

# *Songs Of Belonging*

•

*...the heart refuses to be imprisoned;*
*in its first and narrowest pulses it already*
*tends outward with a vast force and to immense*
*and innumerable expansions.*
                    —Ralph Waldo Emerson

# Crowd of Absences

Ornate statues green-black with age,
their mouths waterspouts, their poses
a continuous flow like the water in
the basin and all around them;

skies absorbed, mounted militia,
the closeness of lovers passing by:
the musings of ages collected
stir in those who stand there

and listen to the fountains rushing.
The idea of nothing need not
occur there, and if you are alone
it is quite another condition than

being alone in a crowd of
absences. What can they provide?
Nor can you by yourself replace them.
Only an accumulation of lives

—in casts poured long ago,
in fields pondered for as many lives—
can free the heavy need in you
for breaking out
to survey—expand expand—
and yield to song.

# Songs Of Belonging

*A Sequence for Hanna Axmann-Rezzori*

## The Rising

We landed

and like a flag hoisted in the wind
you rose

looked out again
across a terrain
vast
various
human

and soon recovered that sharpness
keenness of perception
with which waterbirds view
sleek targets
swift and shimmering

naturalness
strengthened you
shadows soon filled
their spaces

and you knew
that everything you looked at —
the dry riverbed
cars and motorcycles at
the railroad crossing
the lighthouse
the coast of the South
the innumerable tiny shells
on rocks in the shadow of rocks —
everything was connected

a fabric like one
of sunlight
of water
of air

a fabric behind which
shines a face

endless and enduring

a face
that had beckoned you too
to rise

be you again

all of you

the sacred
and the less than sacred

# To Be Part of

To be part of
the ebb and flow around you
no more no less
than waves are of the sea

to be in the houses and the trees
the lawns carefully kept
the flowerbeds
round metal bars between
the grass and gravel paths

to be in the things around you
as much as the things you love
are in you

to feel that the world breaks into you
as music does

the people on iron chairs
the people on the paths
the people at tables outdoors

and the birds that fly up
between the trees
and the sky between trees:

you know then
you are where you are meant to be
are as you are meant to be
in this human climate

happy
or sad

# The Loire at St. Firmin

A silkenness
of flow
water
air on water

a silkenness by the river

like lace
the foliage across

even the trees
conform to human size

as do the steeples
characteristic of this region

the black steeples
of churches and chateaux

windows add to
the silkenness

by the light that
accumulates there

light discerned
by attention only

but is there
as surely as the river's flow

the canal's flow across the bridge
where from time to time
black barges add to
the silkenness
a flowing bulkiness

# Hanna's House

Her house is like her paintings

She has brought to both the joy
inherited from stones, old
tile roofs, from church
steeples, walled-in gardens

She has never lost the child she was,
has created this space, these rooms
for it, for the child to be
free, at home and at ease

Nothing in this house could offend
the child

The small pillows all the same size and shape
are arranged on the bed to form a color-blend
of all the shades of blue, and stand
upright like tin-soldiers standing guard
or small columns in a tiny city by the sea

Her pictures of old
stone buildings, steeples
white and gold
(a child's world not lost)
invite the child
to enter

especially the one of
an old chair, a grandmother's shawl
draped over it, both white as
the old age of time, a chair
and nothing else in
a deep space with blue hills

a chair for the child to climb up on,
from there to look out at grown-ups
in that odd old way
only the child has
that has not been robbed
of space


## At St. Benoit

From the gentle countryside
the light through the trees
and on the fields

from the spacious square
the old houses with flower boxes

from the well-kept square
through the large wooden door

into
the large space of the church
into
the dim light
the organ music

into
the light held in
into
the sounds flooding the space

and the stillness

of light
and space

and the whiteness

into
the whiteness
of light held in
of sounds surging
and of the stones

the whiteness of the walls
of water solid, the stones

the whiteness of
the candles slim as
the height of the church

the web of
the arches
way up

the web of
the arches
from the depth
of grottoes

the water congealed, the stones

From
the flow of light on the fields
the glitter of light through the trees

from
the spacious well-kept square
the old low houses, flowers
in windows and entranceways

into
this water congealed
this light
held in

into
these sounds like the
perpetual sound of the sea

into
this grotto under the sky
the light
held in

and the chants
throbbing

## At Sancerre

Whether we drank fresh wine
at a cafe in this ancient town
on a hill overlooking the river
and its tended valleys

whether we remarked upon
the bent old woman with
her shopping bag who seemed
so much in place as we
watched her enter the
pastry shop and leave

whether we noticed that
the street to our right
had been named The Street Of
The Jews during
the Middle Ages

whether we watched late in
the afternoon along the river
maneuvers of two small birds
snatching fish from the river
with incredible swiftness:

we sensed the pattern
was undisturbed
the pattern
long ago established
was as it had been.

And felt this particularly when
driving toward Chartres we saw
the great towers of the Cathedral
rising as though growing from the earth

rising and growing across the fields
like sunrise
across the sea.

# At Chartres

To approach
and walk around
those massive sides
masses of stones
when the great portals
were closed

was like ascending again
at the end of day
to the garden

to the garden with
the well and cowshed
and chair under the tree

Full of a grave love
the expressions in stone
of the faces
the long figures
in the porches and the portals

Unaccountable
the eyes of the dead
that had waited
had peered from behind the leaves
the stares of the dead
fixed on the man below
about to speak.

*Inside, in the morning*

I sat in this immense space upward
the long extended figures
the faces looking down

the colors bright
the faces looking down

I sat and swayed like a child
a child lulled

and I began to remember
  *space beyond memory*
  *sleep beyond sleeping*

the figures floated

the faces looked down

the stones a sheen

# In the Town of Chartres

Like a child for the first time
seeing a tree, bark, a flower
in the wood

like a child looking at formlessness
and the form of things

when the eye is purely what it sees
and nothing intervenes

so was our first look
so did we look at each other...

What can prevent
waves from thrusting themselves
upon each

lovers, face to face, or wrestlers
from rushing
at each?

Nothing can intervene
and nothing did

until we turned

and it was not a calm
but desire
a desired agitation
made us turn

you to your companion at your table

I toward an alien land
days still and many miles beyond

## Quai Voltaire

One last walk
by the beloved river

one last look
at the beloved buildings

the stately buildings
and the gardens and fountains
across

one last look
at the bridges and the river
and the tower up ahead...

Here where I have been so
at home
here in this most human
of habitations
here where I have rested
with the ease of
the many many pigeons
under the many many eaves

this too
dissolves

this too
dissolves even if I did not have
to leave

but O
the faces of the many statues
outside the great cathedrals

hold it, hold this
that I must leave

this that dissolves

and the music
holds it
and the face of the girl playing

and the faces of the people listening

and the lips that cannot find the words


## My Soul, a Girl


My soul
when I return
from where I am at home
to where I am not

is a girl
that had awakened
had smiled
had laughed
singing songs

my soul, a girl
that when we drove through
tree-shaded streets
past gardens, old houses
and people at tables outdoors

had stood up in me
out of me
like a girl standing up
in an open car
her hair streaming
her face joy

my soul, a girl
that when I return
to where I am not at home

sits as though fallen
as though hunched over herself
in a grey space
behind a window with bars
and is ashen
all of her ashen

nothing that happens around me
will rouse her now

only art

only the songs when she hears them

the songs of the great joy of belonging

that she herself has sung

# Val de Loire

They are gone—the golden fields
the blue-shuttered house narrow and white
the bridge across the canal
the country road down where
the village's young cyclists raced
the cattle that stared with dumb curiosity
and kept on chewing as I passed

gone the young swallows
jubilant in their new skill
and forming a swift cloud against
the sky's puffy clouds seeming content as
the sitting cattle in the fields

gone...
The silence each contributed to
the tall wheat humming in the golden fields
the line of cyclists caught in
the unruffled surface of the smooth canal

the condition that can never change
that each thing in the open air gave off
like moist scent from trees, from fields:
words of welcome, home, return
at the core of every sight perceived...
gone,
changed for me now
silence, whispers, permanence.

# Abundance, Now

1.

Out, I seek nothing
knowing that no sudden wind
no sudden apparition in
the empty street

will bring a classic hill-land back
temples atop steep slopes
philosophers and their
young disciples in a market place,
amid crafted marble in a bath.

2.

Abundance, now, must go unclaimed
must wear itself out
like any storm, must wander about
unknown, unseen, at best
a memory of bright exchange
as when one light lights up another

for those who reached out and
—startled—held, beheld: for them
at most a memory to ponder.

*Three*

# *Embodiment*

*A Meditation*

●

*Once again, to Hanna*
*in whose little salon in her house*
*in St. Firmin-sur-Loire,*
*in the summer of 1977, this poem*
*was first conceived*

# I Nearness

1.

I sat late in the sunset
on the terrace of the cafe facing Estoril's Casino garden

before me, on the lawns, between trees,
along the gravel paths
human figures standing, waiting,
darting back and forth

driven by restlessness
—as of youth, or of
the weather stormy for days—
driven to find what?

The sun almost descended across the coast,
the melancholy of the familiar
took hold of me

sights familiar as
the familiar sights
of home

hydrangeas so full
the heavy bulbs fell apart on the lawns

sights of
white walls, tall windows, narrow balconies

the entire sweep of the coast
a reach of arms to receive those
who return by sea after many nights apart...

all near, all close again

all near, all close
but no more held by me
than is the sea by rocks,
the entire scene so familiar
but no more held by me
than is the sea by sand
the water reaches and as in
a full embrace, covers for a time.

2.

What was it they wished to find, to face?
wind and light and dark flapping between the trees,
the flutter of leaves like a flutter of wings...

What were they wishing to come upon
within undulations near yet vague,
near yet vague as the light of
the moon, as night across the waves,
as the desire that alternately soared in
and sped from their hearts?

A face that has in it
their own degrees of want
— unbearable, intense —
but has in it as well
a distant, cool disdain?
At once contains
their want of passion
and the promise of the calm that follows
like that of snowy peaks climbers reach
beyond the fear, the blinding climb
through clouds?
The expression itself,
the face without features it contains,
contains though hidden as if behind fine skin
like the rocks of a coast the fog conceals,
a quick break in the clouds reveals?

Were they hoping to find
the expression itself
in a body passionate
yet distant, pale

pale in the first rays of day
as is that light

a body overexcited
perspired, wet
yet pale, the pallor of distance,

pale when morning breaks
pale as the crumpled sheets
hurriedly left in the early light?

3.

Not attached—as the wind,
the shades of dark that fluttered
between trees, trembling streak
of bright fog far out at sea—
not part of the daily routine
that holds back those living there
from the wind, the fog, the sudden
dreamlike features contained therein,

what was it I was close to,
attached to? What was it
attached itself to me,
expressed itself through me
as did the sights that were familiar
close, yet not, sights that
instead of their shapes
cast upon me a sadness
as mourners over mirrors a cloth?

What was it that thrust itself through me
in its thrust taking with it
wiping out my preferences for this or that
so that I was not one sight
not the garden where I sat
not the flower-lawns across from me
not the road along the coast
lit lampposts I could see,
was not the lights across the waves
not the figures waiting
not the figures darting back and forth

was not any one of these
not any one more than the next
not one but every one of these

was, had in me, what
the searching figures—
whether they were standing under trees
or fled across the grass
pursued or in pursuit—
yearned, had yearned
with a depth that is age-old
to come upon in the face wherein
what held me as it held them
stirred, beckoned,
ready to break into
expression.

4.

(It was some time later, in the small living room of a friend to whom after years apart, I have for some years now been returning each summer, it was while listening to Bach's Chromatic Fantasy, and in particular, to the passages that take me to the recognition that I seek

—face behind the face, face within the face, place within the place—

it was while listening and watching my friend's newly acquired kitten play with its reflected paw, its body's reflection in a small table made of mirrors,

it was then that this experience of, as it happened, a few weeks ago rose before me, appeared before me in clearing perspective.)

5.

What do they feel
directly after the encounter, consummated, is over

when in the first pale light they steal from houses
the ornate front door shut noiselessly
and they run down the street
to their cars or look for a taxi?

What do they feel
after one more encounter,
after they had glimpsed again
what is unspoilt and never discarded,
having touched again
what alone has bred desire,
to where alone desire leads?

Have they, after the loosening of hands,
after the brief sleep and change
from moonlight to early light of day
on the damp bed, the rumpled sheets—
have they already lost
what they had anticipated so severely,
what, for a while at least,
they thought that they had gained?

Heads bowed, they know only
that departure has been increased,
that what is gained, that gain itself,
that gain experienced, is loss.
That when what they had sought is held
glimpsed like a flicker in flight in
someone's eyes, a mysterious mass
of gold, of white,
a dislodged treasure
or a glacier floating past—

that they know not then
who they are nor whom they hold,
nor what they are when
they and whom they hold dissolve
as the barely visible object dissolves
back into indiscernible distance.

Heads bowed, know only
that loss has been increased,
that in that loss, that necessary loss,
they had touched again what can, if not
be found, be sought as they had sought.

6.

In retrospect
amid glimpses of a kitten playing with its reflection in a
                                                    mirror,
the sequence of events shifts.

The time when I ran down the steps of a theatre before the
                                        curtain fell
because I could not hold back my tears, somehow
                                having sensed at the
age of nine

that love lived is an illusion, a betrayal

and that the drastic act of the betrayed to annihilate
                            what had betrayed her
—her body, her life in the world—a noble sacrifice;

that time when I had gone to the opera, the *Volksoper*,
                                by myself on a
Saturday afternoon
and for days could not hum "un bel dí" without bursting
                                        into tears,
is out of sequence now.

Directly behind the scene of the boy
storming down the theatre's marble steps
hearing the heroine's last cry
as he runs into the crowded street,
is the man of thirty, forty, fifty.

Countless incidents flash by,
each a tried, a failed attempt
to hold on to what cannot be held,
to bring into the realm of time
—into the body's closeness, touch of
the ear, shudder of nakedness—

that which glimmers, glitters, beckons
but will not be trapped in time,

for whose sake lovers have turned into trees,
have dared the underworld, have lost what an
unblinking eye would have retrieved,
have feigned poisons and staged a mock-death;

for whose sake men and women have given up
the world, have handed their parents their
clothes, have slept with the trees under snow.

7.

A night a few days before Christmas
at a performance of *L'Enfance du Christ.*

A choir of angels accompanying the *Flight Into Egypt,*
the tenor's aria perfectly appropriate for
the announcement of love. No conflict, strife,

no selfish motives, only
harmonious entry
a ceremonious walking together

movement without moving as though
those on their way moved onward
by clouds and a glow above them
and the voices, an amen, from afar.

Love's reality
no different for me then, at thirty-five,
than it had been at nine,
or at nineteen when

looking up one day in class
I had been startled to find
love's expression staring at me

the look I've often since caught
in eyes, desirous, capable,
or in paintings in the face of
the lover, or of the mother,
beholding the beloved.

8.

Or earlier, at twelve,
when sitting atop the leather practice-horse in the
                                        gymnasium
and leaning against it stood the boy who had been my friend
but whom, for no reason that I could understand, I had told
to go away
one afternoon as a group of us walked home from school
down the park's tree-lined wide gravel path

and when I looked at the boy standing there then with
                                        arms crossed,
one foot on the shin of the other leg, and leaning against
the practice-horse stood there poised, posed like
an oriental god or athlete in classical times,

I felt then as I looked at him from where I sat
—and know now that I saw him then as
the totality, an early experience of
the one expression

the one expression I have found again and again
in many experiences since

realizing now that even then
I had faced nothing but the one
apprehension of the one face

the same face, face without
features, smile of heaven
in faces of stone, in the many
experiences I've had since
of confrontations and of bodies held:

know now that as I saw him standing there
as though he had been crafted, had been
created as a symbol to remind us of

perfection, but of frailty as well
—for he moved, stepped away, changed
his pose; for he had looked at me
when I had told him, unaccountably, to go
away, had looked at me then with
non-comprehension, hurt, pity—

know now that as I saw him standing there
in all completeness as if for an instant
he had existed outside of time

that I felt then as if I had for the first time looked
at completeness in human form.

9.

To touch completeness

and is it anything else the spirit desires,
the spirit being capable of the shattering moments that
    follow completeness recognized, reached, for, touched,
the spirit being capable of letting demolished experience
                                                    settle?

As, thunder rolling in the distance,
blossoms of wildflowers scatter and
litter the grass and bushes along the path
we take on our walk to the canal
once the enormous clouds the color of elephants
have rolled across;

as the old stone house and the earth around it
withstand the weather
so can the spirit take
the aftermath of experience
as long as it is that of
completeness
or at least
of the connection to it,

for what else does the spirit desire
(I ask myself as I listen to Bach
and watch the kitten trying to catch its own image)
but the expression of its own
capability —
the expression like a face in water —
what but its own reflection
and, in sights come upon,
sounds suddenly remembered,
the memory of home?

10.

Completeness...

is it not that
and that alone we seek to recapture

for its moments restored to us
that we turn backwards
seek out the dark to countenance
its aliveness, shimmer
and unmistakable style?

Islands drift past like clouds,
houses forming clusters around palaces,
temples, monasteries on mountain peaks
along rivers, cliffs along coasts;

the formal gardens we played in as children,
the popular amusement park where
when we were boys we first sensed that
the impossible can be pursued,
the intangible, intractable held
as we watched figures disappear behind
trees into the sunset;

histories we read,
lives of cities we imagined,
were reminiscent of it,
as were the sunny lawns
where bathers tanned themselves and lounged
when suddenly a coldness fell,
flocks of clouds driving across.

11.

And so we think of harmony,
of the outlines of completeness,
only as we remember it,
for to have a sense of it
do we not have to have known it?
And we did. Do when
the experience that embodies it
has passed
as we set about retrieving
through the flesh.

We stand before a painting.
We are amazed at the skill, the light
captured in a room on canvas,
the depth of understanding in a face.

We may be overwhelmed at a concert
by the statement only art can make,
but know it must be through the flesh,
have, if we're honest and not afraid
to admit it, sensed at least once
with a strength not to be ignored,
a lure not to be forgotten,
that it must be through the flesh,
a total engagement, nothing less,
that we retrace the past to where
our loss began, to desire's origin.

12.

Bodies, bodies...

To sense for the first time
the singular excitement of

embodiment, the one temptation

to sense for the first time
this truth of the body:

that what to us is most immediate, private, mysterious
but separates us
is also our most direct means toward

completeness.

Imagine a boy taken for the first time
to a famous bath. He watches the bathers, young and old,
ascend the broad steps in a park-like setting
as he descends to the wide and sun-drenched grounds.
He has put his clothes in a locker,
his older brother who brought him
has gone to the pool. The boy is on his own
and is drawn by the silence and brightness
to the lawns behind the locker rooms.
A sign tells him these are the sunbathing grounds.
Shading his face with his hand
he sees, and this for the first time,
not a boy his age but a young man, a stranger
fully naked in the sun, the man's whole body
stretched out in the light, in the heat
as though in an act of yielding, as though in an—
to the boy not yet experienced but already
secretly familiar—amorous intent.

And that mysterious something that the boy
has always known though not yet
observed, not yet experienced, that has lain in him
hidden, as yet unsummoned, known but
forgotten as if on thinking oneself lost in
a dream there appears before one
around the corner, deep in the garden,
the white walls and shuttered windows,
one's home behind the trees:

that mysterious something once stirred, as then it was,
never again to be ignored
will from then on always seem
to glimmer just ahead of him,
in someone else's eyes, behind
another's skin, yes, awaiting him.

And it seems to him as he watches
the bodies by and in the pool, in the steamy air
their movements as in a private ritual, ritual
dance, that this it is, this
privacy, hidden splendor, this
the secret language that the body has.

13.

Through the flesh that we move backward
and thereby ahead to what awaits us,
through the flesh that we find again
fine tracings of the beloved outline,

by moving through the flesh as though
our bodies were the landscapes of our lives,
that we come again upon, come as far as
the threshold of the one perfect vista...

As, on at last entering the building
we had first heard of when we were children
—columns, cornices, roofs becoming
firm realities in our young, impressionable minds
and later as adults in our dreams—

having at last come close to the hill
on whose top the glorious edifice rises,
the ancient halls of the ancient gods,
having at last reached the steps that ascend to

its beginning, ascend to the vast plateau
where one approaches, as in Rome across
the enormous square, St. Peter's,
the entrance to the homestead, residence of
the gods that in its enclosure contains
dimensions suitable for the invisibles to

be striding in: having beheld it first from
a great distance as a devotee might
after wandering for days and
early one morning spotting it,
seeing it grow out of the sparse fields,
the vast parched plateau, out of
the distance like haze as if it were a cloud,
the first cloud for days in a burning sky:

having seen it first in its completeness
as we approached it, and, as it has been there
for centuries, returning to where celebrants
once had immediate contact with what is
at great remove for us
and we may now hope to get close to
by reverse traversal through the flesh,
returning to the steep steps
we may now be ascending for the first time. —

And then, as on at last entering
where we have for so long belonged
and walking down the wide floors
paved with large rectangular stones
set at different angles so that
the entire floor is a vast stone mosaic,

we come at last, having retraced so much
we had heard and dreamed of, come at last
to the structure's farthest line,
its end or its beginning, depending on
one's approach up the hill, come at last
to its vast openings, we had observed
the outlines of mountain ranges gain focus
between the columns as we crossed the floor,

and, as we lean against the ornate though
broken stone-slabs that connect the columns,
see from there as though the building had
contained it, had brought this within its
space surrounded on all sides by columns

like walls: the hills beyond...
the darkening shapes of mountains beyond the plains,
see now contained within this contained space
the land-shapes and the colors we remember:
the distant hills and shadings
we associate with home.

14.

Here, then, where I return each year,
in this house, this modest building,
in this room of modest size,

here, where I sit and ponder
what the expression contains, expresses,
the music starting to fade into
the silence it is built on
like waves that flatten into
the sea's vastness when the winds die down —

here, where as I sit
the kitten has not yet tired
of trying to catch its paws in the glass:

how, I say to myself,
how, without the body, can the spirit
know its features, delight in what it has
created, test how extensive are
its capabilities? How, without
structures, buildings, can love
be stated, contained, expressed

when there are no doors
no rooms wherein to dream
the rooms of our dreams,
no beds for the return we make
each time we lie down to sleep?

I walk out on the balcony. Below me
is the small walled-in garden,
beyond it the walled-in gardens of
other houses, the low, tiled roofs
of the simple cottages where
men and women have lived their lives
rising from and returning to
their simple beds in the dark,

beyond this cluster of houses
the fields, the cattle,
the birds that lift from the roofs and trees,
and beyond, atop the distant hill,
the ancient walled-in town, its ivy-
covered walls, ramparts, towers inhabited by
white pigeons that prefer the town to the hills and fields
                                                    beyond,
that fly up from the stone-basins and sit
in the narrow openings in roofs and turrets
where they return to sleep:

through expression alone,
by what other means than embodiment
our sense of the inexpressible,
our glimpses of its features

in the tree, the roof,
the town preserved up above

in every column, cornice, pile of stones
that create the space wherein
the sacred is enclosed, contained
atop the hills the ancients praised

sacred...
body, flesh by which
the sacred lineaments are glimpsed:

body we travel through, traverse
in the attempt to reach...

15.

You, or however that is referred to
whose features that are never traced
each face set on its pursuit contains,
you who glimmer in each face wherein
the dream of your appearance is retained:
once you have been glimpsed within
the darknesses that alternate with passing clouds,
who has ever forgotten you?
O you! One face within each face!

One form within the planes and angles,
multi-dimensional shapes and
habitations, architectural splendors,
invisible spaces rooted and grown
in these: you, without whose abstract
though clearly beckoning glance I do not
exist, amongst whose striding gracefulness
I plead to walk: be near! stay near!
Contained! retained! expressed!

## II Departures

1.

I speak of nearness because
I have never lost sight of
the dangers of severe departures,
have felt in my blood the pulls
that lead us into wastes

—outcasts there,
exiled, head bowed, naked
and ashamed of our nakedness—

pulls that take us into regions
beyond the boundaries of return,
into barren stretches so disordered
it is impossible to maintain
a sense of the right direction
so that return can no longer be
accomplished, requires the highest
intercession few are qualified to request,
repentance of which few are capable.

It is true of course that those who
have reached there, have arrived there
(albeit unknown to themselves) out of
a thirst for no one but you, for nothing
but you, or him, or her, or however that
whose features we are above all
enamored of, is referred to.

But the pursuit of a noble objective
is noble only if
the objective is clearly held in mind
and a view of it,
an ever greater closeness is the aim
and not the physical excitement
encountered on the way.

Wanting this and not the clarity beyond
for which the tempting body is merely a bridge
is a departure akin to
falling into a state of drabness

stretches of fog or of steam drifting,
grounds littered with
crumpled papers, pine needles, dead cones;

caverns
whose walls of damp stalactites or congealed roots
one comes upon with hands stretched out
to feel one's way,
for the fumes, the vapors, the drifts
make it impossible to
discern anything but
the grossest outlines:

bodies, yes; features, no.

2.

I know, for I have been there.

And those of you who have not
if what you pursue is indeed not
visible form,
unable as you have been,
unable as you are to rid yourselves
of the nagging truth that
the body's appearance is little more
than quick apparition:

if what you pursue is
the steady grandeur, closeness, sheer love
only the visible can
suggest and reinforce
in your desires and your hearts,
you will have to pass through there
if you are not afraid, not ashamed
to admit that it is not the flesh
but the features in the flesh,
that it is the spirit
you pursue. Otherwise

you will remain there,
will join those who gather there nightly,
and soon will have little else on your minds
for you will have come to assume
that the excitement, the fantasy
acted out there is real
and any other interest
—desires and needs for the invisible—
unreal, unworthy.

Whereas
where you will be gathering nightly
is in fact not a place of enjoyment
—you are not pagans! yours are not
pagan rites!—but
a burial ground you will find yourselves in
when it is not the bodiless features in the body,
the structures atop hills in the sun,
but the body itself,
the body's nakedness of which you have become
ashamed
that has lured and led you

and after some time will claim
that you no longer remember
what in fact the body's nakedness suggests:

pillars, spacious
courtyards atop hills
stone-white and naked in
the sun

—grounds in every way
different from
where you will then find yourselves.

3.

Arms thrust out like dogs pursuing a scent
ready to tear off a trouser leg,
but they who come there nightly
do not know who he is
—or who she is, or who you are—
assume he is one of them,
the one they've been waiting for,
whose aloofness when he does enter
and crosses the cavernous rooms
they accept but not that they
are struck by him because
he is everyone's memory of
the redemptive figure alive in each,
the radiance in the flesh
each remembers even if never met.

And for an instant so brief,
a glimpse so quick, so deep
they are not aware of it,
stand transfixed, enraptured by
his royal shadow blue as
a mantle of air, by his silence
that by its power, the power of music,
could change a river's flow,
could shift rocks and alter hills.

Barricaded each night in pursuit of
what they've been led to believe they
must have—protracted happiness,
godhood on their own personal terms,
nothing less—desire aroused in them
now like a vengeance, they reach
to grab him, try once again to take him,
arms outstretched surround, implore him.

And they are an outlandish lot, many
among them men as women, women
as men, who turn on him now
as though still roaming ancient Thrace,
still howling across its wild
solitude, still bloodying
the waters, driven still by
an ancient hunger and an ancient fury
to tear from the holy favorite
the melodious, godlike limbs.

4.

There

where there is not
the memory
of steps and songs
across crests of the land

of light-footed love
that enlists and subdues

not the memory
of fierce eyes driving
the presence of heaven
into the soil

of fierce eyes lifting
hearts and fields to the sky
brothers and bridegrooms
of love and the poor

there

where no procession of men women and children
dragging stones for the walls on the summit
to embody the love that
has passed there
sings

there

where nothing reverberates

where nothing remembers nothing

5.

Not to care, not to see, not to heed
the silent messages images reveal,
illumination inherent in every thing perceived—
"light of consciousness in all thoughts and
perceptions"—
the high pillars atop high grounds
casting around them a whiteness
a light more intense than
the chalky whiteness of the stone they're made of,
light perceived less directly than
the glow of the sun on the stones—

not to heed what images illuminated tell us
the expression is an expression of...

Though this of course not in words but
proddings, cryptic signals,
guideposts that indicate
not arrival but the pathway ahead
like the wooden poles hung now with electric lights
with lanterns in former times
that give direction to boats
heading out of Venice into the lagoons.

Not to care, not to attend, to forget
that whatever occurs within time
each phenomenal manifestation
is extinguished as candlelight in a wind
or because the flame has come to the end of the wick,

that the image of a runner, of any athlete
when shown on a screen moving across a field
in slow motion, every movement
an expression of perfection
as though classical statuary
had come alive for a moment:

that even that
caught in minutest motion
enlarged and slowed down to almost a halt,
that even that
is illusory
for the moment after it appeared
it is as though
—as a wave receded back
into the flatness of ocean—
is as though
it had never been

water now
water now, water
nothing but water.

6.

To illustrate this principle
that is absolute
expresses itself all around us
but is nonetheless
not heeded, ignored
causing in consequence
the ills that result from
stubbornness
and an accumulation of lies
causing in turn a fouling of air
as, for example, in rooms where
everything the people who lived there ever possessed
is kept
paper, paper, paper,
old shoes, spools of threads
and boxes, boxes
and everywhere over everything
the feathers from pillows and feather-beds worn to shreds
as though in addition to the owners
geese and fowl, long dead, had lived there.

To illustrate the folly
full failure of responsibility
when what is so obvious, apparent
and all around one
is ignored, refused acknowledgment
with arrogance, stubbornness

and the birds, a black mass of birds
hunted and distraught in
a smoke-like sky,
distressed by an unnatural roar all about them
but not sensing where it comes from
instead of flying away, fly straight into
the death engines,

the birds seem to be saying
their mass death is proof of
how serious is this refusal,
this stubbornness to admit:

*the invisible, the invisible alone*
*is the visible's truth and vitality*
*the expression, the expression itself*
*is never yours*

*you do not, do not have power over*
*what you have not created*
*and you will never possess*

\* \* \*

For example, you have gone back
to the darkened rooms where your parents lived
and while trying to decide
which of the contents to dispose of, which to keep

you have come across a drawer full of photographs
all mixed up and strewn about like torn bits of paper,
pictures of friends and of members of your family
at various ages, at all sorts of places and
occasions. You look at them, at the way
people were dressed, and you remember
many of the places, the gardens
in the country, in the spas,
the fronts of houses in your native city,
the parks, monuments, familiar streets.
And there you are
on a frayed snapshot
in a broad allée in the park near where you lived,
posing with your grandmother and two uncles, her sons.

You no longer live in that city,
nor in that country,
nor on that continent,

more than your childhood
a blur in a fog. All gone,

people, poses,
the expressions on their faces
so fixed in the moment
in what they must have felt just then
or tried to show they felt:
the ordinary, familiar sense
of appearing secure,
for they did have a sense
of who they were
and where they belonged.

You shut the drawer. You will deal with this
later
and, seeing before you
so many lives as nothing but
a blur, a dust,
a dream held in your hands,
you turn back
to the darkened rooms.

7.

When the substratum never visible
is not attended, neglected

when the pursuit of personal interests
is promoted ahead of anything else

when basic realities are treated
as though they do not exist
because they cannot be measured
cannot be seen as visible things are seen

the resulting neglect
settling everywhere

sadness that then prevails
all too abundant despair

when not even the memory of
sacred content, the substratum attended
by means of language, symbols in stone,

ceremonials, robes, processionals,
the sounding of bells,
is alive and retained

as here in these parts it still is
in buildings and often
in faces come across
in busy streets
or in lofty interiors
on benches
subdued, heads lowered.

8.

Out in the garden
the thick hum of summer insects engulfs me,
silence I wade into gladly,
sheer being that holds me
absorbs me like a love,
everything here having once been unified
as though long ago this garden, the hills, the walled-town
                                                    up ahead,
the roofs, yards, the trees scattered below
were merged, held in a oneness
achieved by those who had walked across the land
singing creation's song.

A quality, this, akin to that
expressed by statues of patron saints
in church portals and walls surrounding medieval towns
                                        along the Adriatic,

figures representing true patronage,
statues of saints cradling a model of the town they protect,
the town unified and held as a single object
in their arms: oneness
inherent in embodiment,
expressed by figures in a humble pose:
love of which
this countryside having once been absorbed in it,
once held by it, still dreams.

# III Return

with *Coda*


1.


Whiteness
as day descends,
whiteness
of statuary in the open air,
of walls, flaked portals,
of sheets hung up to dry,
of strips of cloth around mummies,
whiteness of shrouds.

Sleep has descended
on birds, rodents, insects,
on tiny almost invisible creatures
deep in the dense tall trees
below on the way to the cemetery.
Flowers have closed their petals,
buds drooping from stems
like the heads of people
dropping off to sleep
standing up in a crowded train.
Sleep descends, each thing
that lives subsumed by
the paleness that has swept over each
like one vast wing.

Daylight floods my room
as I pull the drapes,
throw open the shutters
and hear the sounds
of birds, of insects
buzzing in the garden
and below in the fields.

Where? Where had I gone?
From where have I returned
when on waking, on coming back
I feel as one does only when
at home,
a confidence akin to that
of birds in flight,
of flowers raising themselves
and opening their dewy buds
to the ascending sun?

2.

The picture around me is
complete, achieved
as breath at full peak.

From the clearing in the garden
where I lie on a canvas chair

(and I am reminded of
the many times, crossing the Atlantic,
I lay reclined in one like it, watching
the rise and fall of the waves before me,
aware of and waiting for the rhythmic return
when for an infinitesimal moment
the chair is perfectly still and stable
as though afloat beyond gravity)

from here as I turn my head
I see the ascending terraces,
flowers, trees arranged in patches,
houses interspersed between
gravel paths, trees and flower beds,

looking ahead of me, I see
the earth falling off, descending toward
the beaches I can sense from
the faint sea-smell,
from the vaporous strip of blue that rings
the horizon, turning it into a haze
as if in a watercolor distant blues
had been joined into a blur:

a view all around me
of ascending, descending sea-alps,
steeples and ramparts on ridges,
birds twittering, chirping
at intervals precise and measured as breath,

cars speeding up and down the hills
as if in an unannounced race:

a picture whole, complete,
achieved as if painted,
as if reflected in a cloud,
a moment of
the perfect breathing of the perfect machine;

and it is not too much to claim
that as I lie here I can hear
the beat and have a sharp visualization of
the harmony so near, so close
it slides off as dream does,
as water and the air we part.

## 3. *(Coda)*

To be touched by completeness

to be secure again in the knowledge
that where we were, where happiness is,
where in the first light we saw
the first tree, first face,
for the first time the river
fading out into water among trees
into a distance ringed by mountains

to be secure again in the knowledge
that the condition of oneness
is ours still, so close, so near
it seems out of reach, is unchanged
for us now, forever, "this is
the use of memory: for liberation"

to be secure again in the knowledge
that where we were is where we are
and that melancholy arises only
when we imagine separation
where there is none,
when we seek from fleetingness
conditions it cannot give
and we have lost the right relation
to the one condition that is:

the condition of presence
that the body carries,
that broken remnants,
artifacts of the past
contain only vaguely
but in the human body—
once discovered
like a spring sparkling and
unceasing even if hidden—
is unimpaired, is total.

\*  \*  \*

To be touched again by completeness

and how, since it is not expressed
as any one form, any one object
—stone-urn, flower-enclosed terrace
up high enough for a splendid view of the sea—
is not confined
to any one object, any one place

how else should we know
to attempt to touch completeness
had we not been touched by it already

had we not sensed it
infused in an early encounter
of amorous potential
or in a view we might suddenly catch
from the flower-enclosed terrace
of a glistening sea

had we not been touched
embraced by it in dreams
convinced on waking we had known
bliss, and what but
the bliss of completeness could it have been?

We are part of it then,
it has already touched us
lives in us
and since we have known it
and cannot escape the memory,
are driven again and again
to seek out the forms it inhabits

and driven to experience it once more
wait under trees
dart back and forth across flowered lawns,
on gravel paths of a park
late in the sunset

or travel great distances
to seek out and stand
within enclosed spaces
that contain and honor it still.

\*   \*   \*

That we have encountered it again
have been touched again by completeness
we know if
when coming upon the forms we desire
there rises out of us
the condition of presence
so deeply desired, so powerful
it wipes out while it lasts
our sense of separateness
holding the two of us embraced
as if it too, the intense, ignited,
albeit disembodied spirit's love
were a physical body.

And we know then
that we have experienced again
the bliss we remember,
know this
once the pursued occurrence is over
and for a day or two following—
for, alas, it withdraws from awareness,
recedes, departs for
the zones we have no notion of—
we walk about startled, alert and
self-confirmed.

*Four*

# *In Nature's Trance*

•

*Erde, ist es nicht dies, was du willst: unsichtbar*
*in uns erstehen:*
　　　　— Rainer Maria Rilke

(Earth, is this not what you desire: to become
invisible in us?)

The Károlyi Foundation, Vence, July 1980

# A Week in Vence

1.

During the first day
participant in
a union around me,
flower to light, to sun,
sun to flower,
· all over the earth
a felt though invisible
arm
upward the visible
branches and stems,
yellow buds, yellow broom
turned up, tiny bells

praised and blessed
the crossings over
the crossings back and forth
blessed by
the extended
involuntary hand

ii.

During the first night
beholder of
the unexpected child.
In dream's soft
kernel, the lily's
blossom on a stem.
"Likes to be stroked
across the eyes" the mother said —
she who in real life
had led me, a grown man, like
a child, to *there*

where all joins,
everything living flows
to be joined. To the
benign effusions. Blue
descended. From *there*
to here. From *that*
to this. "He dances"
I said as I stroked the child's lids,
"dances, invisibly, for joy!"

2.

Turbulence,
necessary turbulence
the fragrant meshings,
air-sheen, stirs.
Syllables, the best
of bird-songs I heard
on waking here,
consummation's nectar
that increases air's
denseness,
are also wanted
in the cave
the joined effulgence
lifts away from, will
not penetrate.

Caliban-like, the dark
element raves, seeks
to thrust its vital wrath
into the earth,
oozing darkness into slime
that creeps, the crawling
things...for Caliban
what else to couple with?

ii.

Pulls down, pulls down,
to be spilled across,
infiltrating the earth
as dew, as water does,
pulls toward earth
as toward the body on the bed...

poorly you have managed
to remain where
you wish with all, yes,
with all your soul, to stay!

And the other
—unseen, unfelt—
the nod within
meaning *thou art
content*
the instant followed by
the unmistakable smile,
the assent, radiating sheen
that you contain just then

can you endure it,
the lifting force,
not swerve from there
yet go about doing as
you must?

3.

The second night I dreamed again

that my mother who has died, in the dream has not, but
has separated herself from us, has led a life of her own,
away from us as though I, her son, did not exist, has led
her life in some distant, or distant part of town.

Now I have found her again, this stranger who was once
my mother, and pain wells up as from pain's origin, and
I accuse her (why? for having made me flesh?), pour out
my hurt

at having only loss
and not the happiness, my right, my due:

the grounds, the towers of my rightful state,
nothing but a sketch in my mind,
nothing but an ache...

I am like the visitor in a museum who
coming upon a landscape
recognizes in the garden, in the house, in the blue hills
                                                    beyond,
his own true home
torn from long ago...

4.

Torn from where there is no differentiation
though it is there the perfect planes arise,
corniced high roofs, stone supports of a
circumference wider than the reach of arms;
there that the harmonious proportions originate
painters and architects have established
in honor of the eye's capacity also
derived from there, its flair and
grandiose imagination visualized:

torn from the heights that give
imagination its lure and space,
from there to the narrowed, in-
dicated world; from home, its blue
ridges, white space, into the body's
need, the body's turmoil, into the mind's
struggle to recapture the clarity
that glimmers on in memory as here day's
end; into the cry of arms
for other arms, to bring back

whiteness of space, blackness of cypresses,
the, to us, unceasing joy of birds in them
and other sounds of creatures
that never fly from there
like night:

                    all that these
indicate,
all that their sounds and movements indicate
of the one motion, the one sound—

just as these mountains here, poplars in rows,
this sky both blue and white just now,
the barking dogs, the twittering birds
indicate:
            the home

where I return —
undifferentiated realm
behind the names, diverse
multitude of things —
                    the home
where I return
with every thought and breath
— for it is there
                    the one
steadiness —
                    return
to be torn from again.

   ii.

Why, since each sight contains some aspect of
its contours, the roof its cupola,
the stone-wall its column of appropriate height,
          beyond human scale and need —
each column topped by the heads of gods, of goddesses,
their emissaries, winged or in a run;
the stone-wall here its columns in receding row —
the stair outside its wide ascending steps, flight upon flight;
this simple wooden floor its immense open area at the end of
stairs, vast area inlaid with stones, the square leading to
where the blue-ridged distance starts...

why, since the terraced mountain I look out on
is but the slope of ranges ascending into clouds,
to the abode of mountain gods
and of those who attend there
by prayer, still attitude and crashing bells
the presence, constant presence
that, without limbs, descends
among the fields where flowers start, birds wake
with song, among the streets
and into the rooms...

why, since the cloud covering the mountain I look out on
contains as I sit here
gods and their retinue
that step at times
into the bodies of people I meet in a street
or in a garden among slender trees...

why, since bodies I'm drawn to
contain an earth-spirit, fierce and dark,
others a look, an air
come down to them from
the gatherings above...

why,
since nothing, nothing exists apart from its
invisible extension, apart from
contours, countenances I'm free to imagine

why,
as one is of the other

here from *there*

this of *that*

am I not content
with things as they appear, each
separateness?

5.

Flowers are reconciled, or so it seems to us
who absorb their existence as they the light,
wet air they need, in them opposites are

harmonious interchange, earth
into bud, bud into air,
intricate, changing, luminous web,
bursts of flowering boughs, flowering stems,
for us a delight of scents,
leis for the gods invisible,
in stone seated in buddha-pose,
simple bouquet in a simple vase
on lace-covered altar in the
dim chapel ahead, up the road

long-stemmed lilies laid across
and brought on offering arms

flowers as offerings...

Do they too seek to bow before the one thing they are
that never fades, perfect flower, their own eternal shape...
in light always, never a shudder, never a wave?

Do they sense in us
in whom they are absorbed
their own eternal home,
in the changeless root in us, eternal space?
Is it in our extended hand, ceaseless prayer,
that they seek to be consumed

to be forever, single flower,
forever where they are?

If so, shall we accomplish it?
How reconcile the opposites in us
so that we may stand as the one they seek,
toward whom everything living strives,
in whom alone consummation is achieved?

Flower, this, our ceaseless agitation,
no matter what consideration intervenes,
to arrive there, beyond opposites,
to be there, centered,
natural as you are!

6.

Sun after days of rain,
clear shadows on mountains now
where for days clouds had
rolled across, cloud-drifts into
the valleys falling toward the coast.
Now the yellow spotted bushes,
the broom outside my window
bend, sway, reach toward
light dispersed by the dense trees.
No sounds but the slight wind,
bird-sounds interspersed,
the bushes rustling, the broom's
yellow heads swaying like
small bells. Below, the valley is
crowded with olive trees and others of
the South, shimmering branches moving in
the wind like waves. Beyond them,
beyond the tame green, the red roofs
of stone cottages whose white walls
also glimmer in the sun. Here and there
the thick, dark foliage of tall trees
against the mountain's slopes bare,
rock-like toward the top.

ii.

Sun after days of rain
and then
after days of the body's ravings
following my joy in observing
true joinings of earth's growths
with unobstructed light, with
the human presence that
by being reverent, observant,
by being still, by walking down
hills, through fields in this
observant state, may perform,

hand extended, what only it
may do—for flowers, swaying stems,
singing birds, whatever else where
it passes, to come up before it
as if summoned, called to that
of which they too form
an indispensable, in these parts
exuberant, gentle aspect...

following my joy in these
joinings, the body's
darkness stirred,
like Caliban awakened in his cave,
darkness wanting what only light
enjoys...

iii.

And knowing
such is the rule, that light
will only weave and join
where light belongs, darkness
raved for what the dark
may yield. Of extensions none,
none of the vibrant openings
into vistas of light's verve,
into space of landshapes, of
slopes, of bays, of art's perfection.
Of these, none. Only the crammings,
denseness of shrill probings,
slime into slime, denseness of
the body's throbbings, blotted out
the mind, the body thrusting itself
into denseness as though its
boundaries, enclosures
were all, and nothing mattered,
nothing but this, the body's thrills...

until, exhausted, spent, Caliban
withdraws, stretched out, sleeps in
his ooze, his slime.

iv.

              (Dense and clumsy
even the way of putting it.
For how shall language reverberate
where each thing connects only to
itself,
all is dark
and nothing thrives?)

v.

But today,
following days of the body's
ravings — instigating them
by seeking out light's
joinings, light's joy —

today, for me too,
light has woven its wonders,
enfolding me in sleep
with its unique beneficence.
For when I woke
I did not wish to wake.
For where I was
light was endless, so spacious
it is pervasive only there
where sight is powerless,
the ever present calm prevails,
an order of ascents, paths
and heights beyond the mind,
where the eye does not yet have
to wake to the light that must fade,
to the light that will awaken
darkness. And I continued
to linger in this child-like state
—enfolded, embraced
what was I but the child?—and felt
at home, content.

7.

Its outlines, though not defined,
distinct, though not described,
will not leave my mind, its air of
belonging there, welcome complete,
suggestions of its reality here
in views happened on from hills
of bays, of dwellings interspersed,
suggestions of its reality all I
have cared about in scenery, faces,
in words composed, in music, art.
                              It will
not leave my mind.
                  But, flower, fields
filled with the yellow broom,

the consummation you as all living things
strive to achieve, absorption into
the changeless aspect that you also are
and seek in your, creation's ceaseless way,
through human intercession, human evidence,
for how can the changes be enough since there
is pain? the final merging of your endless petals
with the flower ever present, silent
syllables that will be hummed, will it
be once again achieved through us?

Experience tells me, instants I have had of
identity, only if, involuntarily,
the hand extends itself.

              Only when
the body is still as you, flowers,
at the touch of sun, at light's increase
in you, the cycle's grace, and there occurs—
and you have not willed it, and I will not
will it—the moment the body too partakes of

harmonious interchange, when the body
forgets its turbulence and, death-bound,
death-haunted, freed then, released,
is nothing but the essence that you are

only then, for that brief moment
achieving itself and you yourselves
through it, the consciousness
whereby it lives and is perceived:

only then when its opposites that
are never reconciled but can
be cancelled out, are cancelled out

by the one breath, one thing
toward which you lift your stems,
by this
      our evidence
            the hand
toward which you shine.

# The Pine

Alone, here in this wood,
not far from town overlooking
the coast, I say to myself
I must now on my own achieve
identity with the natural things
as in the past I've had
through someone else, with
towns by the water, old streets.

Identity that I so often found
hand on hand, in arms I later
looked at lingeringly as,
asleep, they hung over
the bed's side, the windows open,
the lights on the quai, the dark ships
reflected in the harbor,
the only sounds in the room
the sounds of the still night
and of the breathing on the bed.

Now I must on my own achieve
this union achieved so far through
another, of finding in each other
the belonging we are torn from every time,
the instant of the oneness of things,
the wave being overtaken, subsumed by
the more vehement wave,
the water both are.

                    Outside my door
there is a pine directly in
my path. Day in, day out, at night
listening to it when I wake,
its stillness has been absolute.
I've put my arms around the tree.
Its bark is as firmly part of it
as hair on the human body.

Before it now in the doorway
a few steps away, I try to blank
my mind to really see the tree,
to let it be what it is, to let
it come to me. There is a patch
of sun behind, a large rock at
its base on one side. A bird in
the branches twitters, twitters.

The reality of this, of the tree
and of the things around it,
flows across to me, comes to me
across the pebbly path as

quais, stonewalks, stonewalls,
a face in wateriness...
                    I hear
a song, a voice I cannot trace...

It has been held, all I now hold,
in someone else's eyes.

# In Nature's Trance

In the midst of nature, having come
there drained by the world, its
selfish interests, wearied from all
its wearying effects, worst of all
the grey pall of neglect, I said,
to make my return I would first
reclaim my innermost, most central
cares. Then concentrating there, thought
of little else. But slowly slowly

as though I had lain on my bed in
a daze, not quite asleep, nor quite
awake, and standing all about me,
testing for the right instant to
invade me, were a group of sprites,
teasers, shimmering shades and, who knows,
some angels among them: so did
the things of nature all around me,
move in as though to occupy me,

to claim my inner being for their own.
And without inviting it—and not
knowing it was happening, for it
came about of itself, swiftly as
a strike from the sky—trees,
flowers, wheat stalks, even weeds,
birds, crickets, and so much more
of what I saw and could not see,
had made me their receptor, pre-

ceptor, master as a dog will do.
Then, drawing close around me as if
these were indeed the disembodied forces
that may stand about a brow asleep,

they asked of me I give to them
what they can never reach, the syllables
that float above them, the words that are
the tunes that they have heard like
unsaid whispers, wings of sound,

songs of the very purpose that
they are. Just as clouds stroke the heads
of mountains, so would they have
the hymn of their existence—like
the master's hand upon his dog—
rest lovingly, reassuringly on them,
be uttered where they live and grow,
be blown as once it was when man was
truly at home, their essence one,
by angels all across their valley.

# Improvisation: Among Trees

1.

The child I was when I rode in
the open part of the trolley
down streets lined with chestnut trees,
or the boy when I walked home
from school through the park that had
belonged to the Empress Maria Theresa,
deep tree-lined paths around wide
lawns, ponds, empty fountains,
stone basins filled with leaves...

the child who sat with his grandmother
in the park and would get up to leave,
to give his seat to her friend although
there were empty benches nearby:

I knew then there was a joy
as though I'd come from there,
but also sensed that what
awaited me from then on
as the sun sparkled in
the tops of trees, and I
remember now the clangings of
the trolley on the cobblestones,
was departure's shrill tones.

2.

How little I understood of them
and how real they became when
a boy still, world events looming
above me like the shadows from a beast,
I sat by myself in an express train
at night, feeling the richness of
the trees as they flew past,
their presence and indifference all
at once. Arrived, and sitting by
the lake at the edge of a flowerbed,
I stared at my image, the entire
lakeside reflected in the lake.

3.

This now is my seasonal return.
The loveliness of nature lived with,
aided and loved for so long,
the roses in stone-urns atop walls,
earth's growths cultivated or wild,
vegetable patches, flowerbeds, clipped
hedges, hydrangeas, white, pale-blue:

just as the distant water to the haze
that will lift it into space—
water lifted into blue invisibleness—
so do these hang on to me, to my
capacity to gather them, to take them
into the tones of their completion,
their own intrinsic tones of harmony.

Shall what has not appeared, dis-
appear? joy resident there
be anything but joy? The sea's haze,
earth's garden, our arms, our eyes!
Behind garden walls dogs bark
as I come by. Now, in my room,
I have the chirpings of cicadas from
the bushes, from the depth of trees.

At night the silence—and there is none
like the silence of nature asleep,
tiny swallows, wings pulled in, in
the tops of pines like tiny leaves—
out of its sleep hums to me, lulls me
—silence that out of the sleep
of birds, of trees, awakens me...
not as the man, not as the man.

# For a While, Brief While, the *I*

For a while, brief while, the *I* —
waters coming together at
the same spot that is not
a place, no wetness, only
a haze: behold the fusion,
live nothingness, the glow
of each appearance, each a part

of me: these, my flowers, my trees,
these, my oranges, their meagre
leaves, the fields worked and bare,
the stubs of stalks that hurt
those walking barefoot there;
these, my dogs sniffing the road,
these, my children on their way

for food, and there at
the crossroads, there at
all times, symbol of
obedience, symbol of
my suffering...the sky
my roof, the hills, the cliffs
my walls, the sea my floor —
for a while, brief while, the *I*

# Summoned

*(St. Firmin-sur-Loire)*

Immersed in a novel
— *The American* by Henry James —
I stopped as though interrupted by
a far-off voice. Could the natural
forces — the trees, the sheep grazing
not far from where I read, the water and
its bright stillness — have joined
to call me, lest I be removed too far,
in a time long past, a world by now
no more than of the mind? I put
the book down, went out to where
the water flowed still as in a brook,
to where the trees, mostly acacias,
stood in dense rows forming a tall
leafy wall along the canal's narrow path;
as though summoned went straight
toward them, crossing the cemetery
and pasture on the way.
They rose before me, the trees, in rows
on the steep slope like gothic walls
out of a distance. Like those, on
entering them, the trees, not only of
the wind rustling through their leaves,
but out of their core, out of their height
creating a cathedral dimness, out of
the darkness between them like that
between arches, out of a niche,
spoke a silence human speech does not
match, rustle that is the stuff
of sounds, the gloss of our human
tones. Yet this it was, this other-
than-human eloquence that drew
me there as I had read, that spoke
as though to its own strains in me,
calling me to the one utterance we share.
I stood facing them first, then walked

131

beneath the trees, into their sphere,
as an embrace. The brightness in
the water was the sky's reflected
glare. It seemed to last. I heard
the stillness rustle on and on.

# The Stray

Up on the road I took each day
to walk into town, past views of
the mountains ahead, past walls
overhung with geraniums, at a crossroads
a crucifix, flowers at its base,
a chapel on one corner, a fountain across,
and always at night on the slopes
lights from dwellings twinkling
like stars descended: I saw one night
a German shepherd I took as a stray
going through the garbage pails.
I had thrown out a bone I knew he
would like and I untied my plastic bag
to retrieve it; he took it and
stretched out with it across the road.
When I saw him the following night
he recognized me and, timidly, followed me.

I had been living in the woods
amid haphazard growths of wild
flowers, an abundance of broom,
pines, olive trees. I had observed
ants giving messages to each
or greetings as they passed, and watched
tiny swallows live their shaped lives
among the branches high up in
the pines, had listened to the trills
of birds I could not see, the grinding noise
of crickets in the dense foliage;
after days, after nights had been lulled
by nature's stillness into
a joyous stillness of my own
wherein I was beginning to discern
a common language, vocables of
an order whereon man had shaped his own.

To me it was with an appeal to that
shared oneness that the dog
looked at me, directly at me through
the glass-door that I had closed.
No end was there to the depth in
his eyes that seemed to say to me
that I be a steady reliance to him,
the absolute pivot in his life,
was natural in the natural order
of the connectedness of things.
Indeed, I could almost hear the hum
of this, our common flow. *The love
that runs through us both, through the wood
and every creature in it is*
*the same.* But I could not keep him.
I would be gone in a few days,
and stepped outside to tell him so.
He put his drooling mouth against
my leg. I petted him; I held my hand
upon his head; and then he left.

# The Florist

In the South, in the Alpes-Maritimes,
in a resort of red-roofed residences,
cypresses, oleander in bloom, olive
trees on slopes, clipped hedges, roses,
a young man, in shorts, with sturdy legs —
a local florist as I discovered since —
walked ahead of me, stopped to pet a cat
then went on and waved back to a young
woman on a balcony, probably his wife.
He could have gained something from us both,
for I felt he had responded to me also
but had paid scant attention as I passed.
And he was right, of course. She will
attune him to the landscape, to the
seasonal changes, to his eventual
decline that through her will be
for him a natural phenomenon.
Certainly she will help him in
the cultivation of his plants. And I,
what could I provide? Moments that
flashed through his mind as he selected
flowers for a bouquet, or worked the soil,
sun-drenched and cracked? Images of a
perfection, harmony that exists without
the discords leading up to it? The fruit
without the toil? As I am as he is,
the rare moments a culture embodies
of differences reconciled, sameness
experienced, the pleasures beyond strife
reserved for plant-life and the gods:
such moments humanized, heightened,
personalized: moments that can reach into
the essence of, the timelessness of time?
Surely he has wanted this, as he stood
before canvasses, works-in-stone,
the stillness they contain,

but stood there always in a distant way;
as he looked long and lovingly
at light now on the roses,
light that will be there still
when their bloom is gone,
bare light, light bare as
the mountains behind this town.
To feel assurance then, the joy, relief,
when the cause of sorrow lifts, dissolves;
to experience these moments in
the most intimate, most personal
of ways, he may have missed, may miss—
but can most likely live without.
Not her, whose waiting hands are his.

# The Sheen, *or,* Farewell to Vence

1.

Sheen that comes upon me here again,
that is all I have to rely on for
the sustenance, assurance, assent
I need; amid this goodness of earth,
of man's expression of his harmony
with it, comes upon me here with ease—
the flowers on the steep hills, the red-
roofed homes, slender cypresses, views
from gardens of the sea beyond scenes
of gardens, houses in the distance,
the colors, the perfect perspective
reminiscent of the background in
some Renaissance paintings:—

sheen that here hooks itself into me,
bringing forth its own essence in me
with ease, your reality does not depend
upon externals that reflect you still.
I know that I should do without them,
across the sea, defy them. For I am
but a visitor here, and where I live
the external world does not contain you,
denies you. Will I, when I go, learn
to shut my eyes, cup my hands for you
no matter where I am, knowing you abide
where you abide, that you rise when
and in a way only you can?

2.

Of course I will not deny I miss, that I
will insist reflections of you be
recollected, that you have shone,
that people imbibed your unnoticed
radiance to the great benefit of each,
that it was that, the expression of
that in their lives I've cared about,
sought again and again in others' arms,
blue of your endlessness in eyes,
glow of your benevolence, love's
reality, assent, in lovers' warmth.
Will want to recollect these incidents
on paths like the one I've passed each day,

whose end downhill as it bends one cannot
tell from above, whose gardens, homes
break through the dense clipped hedges and
trees that line the path, in patches
of sunlit walls, creepers, lawns.
In such leafy dimness, changes of light,
I will of course miss intimacies,
recognitions that each time stunned
the face; the silence, deep glow at night,
the different silence of the day,
the sky the blue the depth of the sea,
the single churchbell, distant church-
bell as we crossed the street at noon.

3.

Mornings, on good mornings as I wake
your sheen lingers in my eyes with
irresistible force, of sweetness,
of formlessness, and it is a force —
the senses that take one to where
you begin to be, to present yourself,
the senses that do not define you,

that do not reveal you, contain you—
it is a force, no one can say to me
it is a nothing; it is
shaped, intense, alluring, mornings,
good mornings, no matter where I am;
here, where the things I wake to
reflect it some, across the sea,
where they do not. Only you are
unchanged, contours of your graceful form-
lessness that do not depend on place.
This you have shown me beyond doubt.
As for a while you linger in my eyes,
a moment I take with me into the day
that for at least a time contains
like a river's silkenness your sheen.
Proof that I depend on to be undaunted,
fortified; how else will I dismiss,
defy, and yet live with the emptiness
awaiting me across the sea?

4.

You reveal yourself through nothing but
yourself. Within. From where has grown
expressed in earth, in colors, words,
in stone, your sheen. The proof is often missed,
often slips by, as yesterday would have
in a dim space had I not somehow found
myself in the proper poise. There was a wall
of stone, a window up high, its glass
unpretentious; daylight came in just as
it was; on the wall two slabs of wood,
one nail like a bolt, no covering on
the floor, plain stone: within
that cubicle I knew you shone.

I stretched my arms against the wall,
I felt the roughness in the cracks,
the stones. The senses did not tell me you

shone then, the flow within me did,
the flesh responding to the subtle sweep,
the unpretentious light, the wax
melting on crude iron stands. Later
that day at night, the senses could not
deny you shone. Day's blue had turned
into a glow, the mountains blacker than the night.
Again I stretched my arms as though
the night aglow were a stone wall,
the mountain's luminous rim, a crown.

5.

I know how it will be across the sea.
The soil was never readied there,
the fires never started lie uncharred,
the base materials soaked and spoiled,
exclusive interests in the grossest gains
extinguished them once and for all.
No outward reminiscences of you.
Nothing there is luminous. Visibles,
my cherished visibles, lived evidence
I need and know I shall not have
across the sea, adieu! I wish that I
could say farewell to visibles for good!
For, if I depend on them for

the radiance they reflect here, am I not
dependent then upon those there,
the absence they give off, the emptiness
they spread? I understand, I think, the act
needed to live beyond infusions that
create in human life the closeness that
I shall not do without, to live content
in the knowledge that, eyes shut,
hands cupped, luminousness, although
unseen, is always near. Sheen, sheen
I need you by my side! I know that I
cannot accomplish the attitude,
the constant poise essential otherwise.

*Five*

# The Power of Art

# The Shaper of Words on His Instruction

My response to the perfection of his limbs
—depicted often and more suitably by
painters, sculptors—came less from
personal regard and emphasis than,
I may suppose, a confluence in me
of the voiceless and a voice,
of that which gives its voicelessness,
delight at this embodiment, to words,
and the word-shaper moved to praise.
For what but impersonal permanence
could view and wish to speak of this
creation of smooth flesh as a
mere aspect of the scenery
no more, no less part of it than, say,
a tree, as stable but also in
a ready pose, like a runner, set to go?
What but this supremacy could see
him motionless in motion, his elegance
unfailing and unfaltering,
and ask of the voice it instructs
to overlook, turn from the body's
vehement sexual power that however
alluring and essential to its
full beauty and male worth must end
like any other in the sod, but to sing,
sing of this human form as though
fashioned and unchanging as a god.

# As Though in Pale Morning

The music of existence
the circle of those who lift up
silver horns for praise, for art:
I must be near it

insist on it even if
in lieu of heightened orders
or conventionality not musical
I seek out dark rooms where

men go to retrieve dreams
to rescue parts of meaning
as from a murky stream.
Eventually, if they are lucky,

they stand there—as though
in pale morning
by the water in wet grass—

tonalities
once whole as the complete body,
songs, sensuous, pure as
the body's marble glow,
lifted from the deep.

# The Rooms

1.

Because there can be no follow-up
once each has left the rooms
where what happened happened as though
coming together were preordained,
two interior worlds destined (for
as long as such meeting can last)
to be joined, be entered by each
as though the doors, the walls
were let down like a drawbridge,
a gangplank when the ferry docks,
and artworks stepped out of their frames,
statues from their stone while we
in turn entered their pose, we leave
these premises as dreamers their dreams.

2.

Because we visited each other's space,
each other's sphere of privacy
at will, and there was nothing but
broad welcome on both sides
and desire fell into place like slides
projecting on the darkened walls
pictures that we wished to see
and for a while became; because
possibilities as this, of art
turned back to life are out of place
outside these rooms where we
enacted as on a screen the one
fulfillment the same for each, we leave
these premises as dreamers their dreams.

# Two Poems in Memory of Jean Garrigue

*One*

Snow brings you back. I see
you in your patterned coat
walking toward my building
swiftly, lightly on
the icy street as if a spirit,
well-intentioned and protective
but also urging you to
reflect it dashingly
in how you write and what you do,
had held and enveloped you.

Snow brings you back. I see
you now behind the flakes,
space looking into space.
What held you you have now
become: emblem of encouragement
from high up on the roof
watching out for us
watching out for us who do
not now move lightly on
the street bereft of you.

## Two

Your friend, dead also for some time,
talked of you, and there you were
miraculously before us, nothing but
spirit as you had always been, and
myriad shadowings that form when
intensest spirit and body join. Like
the darknesses among the rocks
enclosing foaming waters, intricate
and clear as that. Whatever the world
had added on to you, what you
had had to take on for survival as
defense, with none of these, only as
you truly were, you stood before us
at the mention of your name.
And when morning came and with it
ready at my bed, day's shields that
in view of how I had just seen you,
your unchanged radiance, turned frail
as any swirling trace dissolving into
nothing in water or air, how sharp
in that first light the boundaries were,
of the unchanging and the changed.

# The Power of Art

1.

The setting is itself memory
memory's stage—
old facades and stairs
archways
to stone walks and steps
to the sea

the town's most imposing secular building's courtyard

well-proportioned arcades
windows ornamented with Gothic tracery

a portico with pillars supporting Renaissance archivolts
capitals depicting biblical or pagan themes

tall candelabra, tall candles flickering
          where the musicians sit

a setting of settings
as though contained in the stones,
shadows and rows of high windows
were the memory of settings—
a precise, a deeply receding
perspective.

   ii.

From the faces of those attending this midnight concert of
                    songs and quartets
it is clear they're absorbed in themselves and the music.

They seem regardless of where they've come from,
regardless of childhood memories—rooms, trees,

parks along canals — they carry with them
             as they do their clothes

they seem to be taken by the music
to the same moment
the same suspension
when the forms of the setting
where they now hear the music
and the forms the setting suggests it contains,
and the memory of settings they've brought
with them shift and merge

and they see before themselves as though through water
the musicians on chairs, the candles flickering,
the courtyard's massive shadows and through the archways
the glimmer of night on the water

see before themselves as though through water
their memories of water
of children buying apples on river-barges

see before themselves as though through water
faces they have loved
the terror and the pity in the faces they have loved

and are brought to the one moment
they will either have to know
or have known already:
the one terror
the same and one in all.

2.

This that you observe,
are meant to observe,
you have not made this

the clearing far in the distance
sky and water glittering
on the horizon

directly before you
below you
the sea clashes against the stones

and you take in both
the light in the distance
the water moody where you stand

and you have made
none of this
                    whose moods
and distant change are yours

and you think of the leaves
as you sat at your desk
and looked out into the yard
on a rainy afternoon

looked with a
caring, lingering
look
at the leaves
yellow and wet

3.

Before the instruments reach
the moment of momentary suspension
in the tumult, the onrush,
the mounting tension

a flicker of clarity
a flash of calm is espied
as though passengers holding on to the railing on deck
                              in a frightful storm
suddenly
          as the ship rolls across a heavy wave
caught sight of

the glimmer
the glitter of calm

a strip of pure glow
way out
way off
in the distance

ii.

When the silence is reached
first of all there comes again
from out of the moonlight
and the glimmer of the sea
that glitters in the archway

a figure
            that steps into the courtyard

moves toward the center where for a moment
the musicians do not play
and the notes are suspended

a figure like an apparition in silver
moving with absolute intent and
inevitability
across the courtyard
across the minds of
the listeners whose eyes
are turned inward

a figure
putting one clattering limb ahead of
the other, not as a man would
but as a skeleton might
encased in
silver armor and mail.

4.

During this part of the stillness
when control
when formulation
ceases

when such realities as:
the bright glimmer on the horizon,
the thrust of the tide in a cavern

enter
whether they are wanted to
or not;

during this interval
when the music pauses—
the music having arrived at, having brought
the audience to the point when

what must come, comes;
what must be, is

and the figure clattering
does the silver dance of death—

who in the audience has not looked back
and seen a beloved city disappear behind
smoke and speed

who in the audience does not remember
hands waving
and faces utterly lost behind
steamed up glass
aware that the burden of water
has come between them,
whole lifetimes wiped out
by the start of a train?

And it is not terror then
not even pain
those who've come, who've been
listening, absorbed in the music
now hold,
            not fear

but a recognition
that shines up toward them
from the depth

recognition

like a stone seething

5.

There are no leaves on the tree in the yard

rain's silver lashings have taken them all

on the brick wall across
the rain has left streaks
irregular as downhill streams

on the radio in the other room
an oboe is playing slow passages by Bach...

You cannot possibly be concrete about
a feeling you loved

an urge that made you go forth
sail forth, reach out
to hold

only that it is gone
what you loved
and is too abstract to name

only that these too are gone
swept away with the silver stroke
when it had to come:

hands that you reached
bodies you slept next to
paintings you stood in front of

and much more you went toward
and can name

settings
Palladian perspectives
the Canal, the Campanile
the Colonnades
the entire huge square
in the rain

   ii.

And you remember this very room
as you stand at the end of the stone-walk
near the steps that boatmen take
and local women use to wash clothes

and you remember how you'd
met whom you'd held, what you'd
heard, what you'd said

and the music, always the music

and the sea clashing below you
against the stones
and as you raise your eyes
far out in the distance the glow
the blinding clearing where
sky and sea having merged
sky and water are no more

6.

In this moment it is not the face of many
not the setting of settings that go back to the time
when this coast was sought out as a refuge
and there was nothing there then but what nature
had formed. But those who then settled there
brought memory
brought to their stones and the land
memories of

rooms, yards,
gardens sloping toward the sea

and as they built their homes
and turned the soil
obeyed them without knowing

memories of views of
white-walled residences,
of swans in inlets

for they could not, nor wished
to drive from their minds
such memories

the sea sparkling below,
the silence of the street
and the annoyance of dogs...


It is then not the face of many,
not the setting of settings, —
it is one face that is there
at the concert at midnight,
the faces of many become one
the memories of settings gone

when it is not music they hear
but the silence the music had
taken them toward

when they see—as though come from
the water that contains so much they
remember, as though drenched in
the light of the moon, in a dance
of silver—this that they will not
escape:

what appears must disappear

who can select what is retained
for who can know how long
in dreams

paths we follow, forms we make?

7.

One face
regardless of the differences
that have made
the look, the shape, the fate
of each

one face—
resilient
resistant to time—
like that of an angel
the face that endures

the face that bears that expression only
once it has recognized
has experienced deeply that

this that is
this that I am meant to observe, to live

this that I now remember:
I have not made this
have had no choice in this

infinite the calm
so far, so distant and yet
the glow across my eyes

close, too close
the agitation of the elements —
arms struggling, cries inhuman as
a doll's thrown to the ground —
about to engulf the path
where I must stand
have come to stand so I
may see, may know: there is
almost at the end of sight
the calm, the blinding glow


The face that states this
is, as if cast in bronze, hewn
in stone,
impervious to
fire, fog, or an
attacking fleet

dreams within dreams it holds

an interior deep as
the universe

mirrors
placed in such a way
that the view of a town in a bay
is reflected endlessly

is retained
the proportions intact
even when

to the beholder's eye
the town by the sea
is a dot, a star
in the depth
the dark of space

8.

In that brief silence
when the figure that entered
that comes when it must
when the figure that appeared
also disappears
and the ghastliness of
dense moonlight dancing in
a circle goes:

then it is that the faces
who've come to hear
the perfection possible in art
are in fact taken there
the instant the moment is reached
that is not time at all

—the silver figure gone
the silver slashings done—

and the faces seem to say
it is then that all creation sings

when that break in time is reached—
time also taken by the silver shade,
that grave necessity—

and there glimmers in each face
the glow that shines beyond change
as though through a crack
like the glow visible in
the far distance beyond
the stormy clouds and waves.

# Muse

I kept close behind
as you whistled me on.
But now across the moody plain
late in the day
I see no tracks resulting from
a horse charged and swift
as though belonging to the sky
no dust from a cone-shaped wind

a conclusion not done...

am I betrayed?

But no promise was made.

# His Departure

He who has lived within you
like an inchoate, inarticulate mass,
he who has been shapeless until
you gave him words —
by giving him contours, tone, musical thoughts,
gave him his landscape,
glimmering horizons and
crossings of luminous seas,
his forward reaching hands,
his voice, his songs;
gave him back his
parks and beloved rooms —:
he has stepped out of you,
has stepped away from you.

Your head turned skyward
you now feel against your face
the disturbance he causes in the air
as he glides above streets
on currents that will take him out to sea.
Left behind, on the pavement
a distance from the shore
you are beginning to discern
the absence that saddens you
as something silken, a cloth,
a mantle made of the sun's, the sea's
metallic glow. You have met
your obligation. He
will meet his fate.

# "So Ist Denn Alles Heuchelei!"*

Tamino, *The Magic Flute*

That each thing evaporates
flowers in late spring
wing aloft as scent
the leaves strewn about
the chance not yet gained
to step back collectedly
and thereby behold
the flower whole—
the bulb like a globe—
the floral shape held together as
a constellation in the sky...

That even stars evaporate
in the endless range of time
in the instant less than time
a star-gazer falls off
to sleep in the grass
and the revolving worlds
have become—who knows?—
a remembered face
widening circles in
a water-surface in a dream...

And so he cried out when
the grounds he found himself on
at a powerful force's request
and by the power of a flute
by blesséd spirits blessed
were not as he'd been led
to believe, sinister, by a
mean pretender ruled
but were gentle, benevolent,
the master's adherents in
each deed and word compassionate.

*(Is Everything Then Hypocrisy!)

This the genius' way to state
that since each single thing in
creation and man-made
does in the end evaporate
and since nothing but nothing
seen felt heard or smelled
is as it appears, and it
is truth and not pretense
those who've set forth want:—
we must in our despair
be thrust back against the face
in our depth receiving all.

# 35 SELECTED POEMS
*1947-1974*

# Blackout

When Europe and romanticism
coasted below resounding blackouts
like an airsick sofa, and Petrarch
sat weeping for wisdom's sake
and the unsung death of lemon bushes,
and Florence coughed out in blood
her ornate fountains of illustrious
merchants, I harbored, O My People,
I harbored mediterranean salons
for white fingers and Scarlatti.

Hitler was an expert at entertaining.
All the world said he was madder
than Caligula. Nevertheless he was
quicker than his own industrialists,
well disposed to great Danes,
and at evening from mountains
pointed out his panorama: smoke
and crematoria, the Simple Right
To Live all gone—and then
"Tara tara tara" on his forest horn.

The sensitive, the disillusioned
in America pantomimed a sad pavane:
Justice dead, the Pure all lost;
and scuttling coffins planted tiny islands
for purity to prosper. It was here
that I looked in, scouting on my life-
boat's murdered rubbish, and it was here
I faced angels on rococo instruments,
saw the grand staircase where
fantastic shepherds rose wet from
a ridiculous sea, memory    memory

# The Chase

In search through gardens, woods,
in sedan, on horse, or foot,
the bird, the goose, the hare,
the jewel in the fish,
the nymph that lingers where
moss and water at the blare
of trumpets, horns, like dreamy
musings disappear: the nymph,
the goose, the bird, the hare
are nothing but excuse
for chasing what is glorious
in all and everywhere.

From *that* to *this* and not
the process turned about.
Why else would hunters bleed
and the hunted sing aloud?

# Basic Movements

1.

He moves out of the dark
unto an empty place
a steersman if you like
at the helm in a fog
and what his mind contains
is more likely than not
at odds with rules of the night
and with a ship's log.

He steps with caution
as though a dancer on
an empty stage in sleep
moving in slow motion
his vision not heeded
ignored by the night
a heavy air settled on
city streets and ocean.

2.

He has moved out of the dark
has stepped forth
has lifted up one arm
the other held stretched out

He has opened his mouth
and not a sound
not a ripple
not a whishing in the air

audible, noticeable, anywhere...

3.

Therefore must love abound
love arrived at when
good attempts have failed,
brave steerings toward
important ends
have been inadequate.
How shall love be traced?
overhung by haze
nothing as its base...

# At Twenty or So

There is nothing will define this look.
How I came to know of it I cannot know
but was more intimate with it, at twenty or so,
than with matters part of my existence then,
and in a clouded distance damp with dreams
saw it, heard it in wild imaginings
along an empty street, a river bank,
or reaching out, face downward, over a brook.

At twenty or so, I was so sure of it
only a lack of testing could have made
this so, and tried in ways I was convinced
I had to take to shape it near my breath,
locked in its look, to force the death
of the ignorance about the thing
I knew so well, for in a visual sense
I was ignorant of its high countenance.

And loved this look that would drive through me as
the first light barely perceptible in a path
between trees, the lightest touch of blossoms
on the faces of travelers still half asleep.
And loving that which would annihilate me so,
it has loved me well, and taught me since:
not confined to a stare or single phrase,
the object and the source of praise,
it is not captured in the eyes it floods.

# Spirits, Dancing

Having put yourself on the way,
it is inevitable that you
should reach here. If in
your thoughts you've had
the notion of reward
as you fought to come this far,
banish them. And,
as penalty for entering,
shed the attitudes of worldly men
regarding us and this
celestial sphere where now
your spirit begs to enter.

From the extremity
to which you've come, you see
us sway as in a dance.
It is no sign that we
are happy. To be happy
is being a step removed
from happiness. Which we
never are. Nor are we sad.
Sorrow is man in the world,
and we, the total expression
and awareness of his state,
are sorrowful.

What seems to you,
who were taught to feel
we must fulfill
where the world has failed,
must turn to good the bad,
must invoke permanence
for material whose law
and will it is to die—
what seems to you, driven here
by urgency, a dance
is nothing but the pain in the world
which we like a mirror contain.

To sway is to depart
as branches from a stem,
as shadows from foliage
thick and dark—
and to depart is what is pain.
What you must know before
you enter this domain
and learn the ways of which
we shall not speak is this
first truth of what you are:
a sorrow, a sorrow
begging for home. Or you
would not have come this far.

# A Single Flower of the Field

A single flower of the field—
one in a great multitude—
not singled out by gatherers
or those who like to speak
of that which is unique,
said to the wind about to tear
it at its root: "Do what you will!

"Your force across this field
stings every vein in me.
Dumbstruck I was when first
you took my pollen and my leaves.
But you have seen yourself in me,
have made me what you are,
and my oblivion has ceased."

# Assisi and Environs

The earth more than the relics
and the timely man-made things—
the land's variety richly
developed, valleys and hills,
cedar lanes and olive groves,
a fertile green differing in tone,
the gentle roads and streams—
the scene unified and yielding like a plant
laden with fruit—painters of long ago
have shown this country so—
arches, water-spans and buildings all
in the same irregular local stone:
the earth more than most other things
suggests now who it was
who once walked over it.

Between the leaves on trees, above
the field where a peasant stacks up hay
while his horses graze nearby
and other fully laden carts
are chased by barking dogs,
between the sight of one such scene
and of another, and between
the bells, the many bells,
the sounds of cymbals hang,
of trumpets and of all such instruments
suitable for the processional,
the timid, unobtrusive passing of
the soul in whom the very soil
reflects itself, becomes itself
as the child coming to life in air.

That such have passed here,
have scattered from their sleeve
of coarsest cloth a wind
of jasmine scent, have reigned
as evidence of what is possible
in man, have dispelled the notion
where they dwelled that man's life
is identical with
the nature of the earth,
have subdued this ignorance
the way an Eastern saint laid low
the deadliest of snakes
by doing no more than lifting up
his hand and walking lightly by
as days go by, and all of time.

To that, to that expression of
the height in man that swept
across these parts as a star
descends across the sky,
to that this land does testify.
Those who seek through living
evidence to understand can catch
between the sounds they hear
the land's perpetual chant
and see beneath the surfaces of trees,
of fields and hills as if beneath a sea
that look of timelessness, of love
in the eyes of those accomplished ones
who walked here once and now still hold
deep in their faces this land, as of old.

# A Tree Unlike Others

There is a tree by the lake
bending way out over the water,
straining over the surface,
like a forlorn wanderer
looking down from a bridge
while most of a city sleeps.

Something so aloof, almost lost
about that tree stubbornly
turning away from others,
patiently straining to see
what others along the shore
cannot catch, like those of us who,
unwilling to linger,
go past and see only
the changes that most of us see.

But the tree has left nothing
behind. Straining over the water,
what does it catch
with endurance and calm
but the image of trees?
And what does it see
beneath the sky in the lake
but leaves and birds on a tree's
bent form, and the leaves
and the birds on each arm
that every season
have come and have gone?

# A Sunbather in Late October

On the bank of the river
covered by a haze as if
there hung a bird—
its head deep in the sky,
its wings so immense
they are always there—
a young sunbather lay
in the dry grass reclined
as on a bed
waiting to submit
to the power of
the autumn sun whose rays
could scarcely penetrate
the veils of thick white air.

From time to time
behind the haze
a ship appeared
whose bulk looked vague
in the diffusing
manner of the day.
No one could say
if men hung in its masts
dead or alive
intent on
spotting the bird
kept out of sight
by the pervasive glare.

In such anticipation
the young sunbather lay
his legs apart
like a woman, enraptured by
the whir of wings,
waiting for mysterious heat
to sting his bones,

for haze to wipe his body out,
for unexpected magic in the air
like a bird with giant beak
to pick his flesh,
eager to recognize his disembodied self
in the mirror blazing in the air!
Why else was he there?

# A Soldier Waiting His Turn
# in a Barber Shop
*(Cadaques, Spain)*

Waiting his turn his eyes
are lost in another's gaze
the mirror holds. They had
not met before. He is a soldier.
The other came from far.

What each caught in
the other's eyes, neither can
explain. It is as if
for the first time, or once again,
they see as man sees man.

Some unconscious gleam
come up like a collect-
ively remembered land,
a peak the sea like time
has kept behind a shroud.

Walks where desires have died,
a height where, like the depth
at which their eyes now met,
thought and heart being one,
the accomplished ones go arm in arm.

Astonished, they are not yet
embarrassed but, as love is fed
by a deep memory
and fire by the things it burns,
cling on to the reflecting element.

But then, and soon, and suddenly as
the recognition came, the spell
that unified them falls from them,
and the one awaiting his turn
now has a look forlorn

as if for the first time
departed from home and cast
into an indescribable mood,
he had for the first time seen
the sea's enormous solitude.

# Runaway Spirit

At night when the streets were still
and most people in the city
had slipped deep into sleep,
a whisper ran down pavements,
air curling like a tornado
whizzing up and down like
a siren or some whistling freak,
a wailing clinging to shut doors,
to windows without life in them.
And this is what it was:
air whining to be earth,
spirit howling for body and face.

And this is what it said,
the freakish thing of air,
the impulse up and down the street
as if it wished to raid
the earth: "Without legs, arms,
without face in the mirror,
without means to attempt
to experience what I am,
without human attributes
what abstract thing am I!
As a tree feels itself most
when a storm tears at its roots,

as lovers who cannot escape the fact
that love expressed must end
love their love best
when they part; as a traveler
seeing an old town on a hill,
bright roofs and towers like a crown
speeding away from him
feels first what he has lost:
what lives knows itself best
when it is suffering most.
It may be odd of me
to demand again the earth,

who know so well its pain,
but when a city sleeps
and I perceive and feel
what is in people's dreams
no matter what they dream,
I turn into a runaway spirit
willing to give all I can
for life in the flesh again."
And so it wailed and whirred,
and all across the city in
the hours between twelve and dawn
this yearning was abroad.

# The Likeness

How can you live, how exist
without assurance of
or at least the memory of
someone, something
fantastic, marvelous
always behind you,
a hand, grip on your shoulder,
a presence surrounding you
as a shell surrounds what lives inside?
Song closer to you than flutter to wing!
Words more antique than age!

Without it—call it intimacy,
your intimate connection—
how do you stand vis-à-vis
the multiplicity of things,
a tree, fence, grass, person in your path?
Unless you find in them
that quality no one defines,
how do you love, what do you
whisper, what song
do you share in the dark?

Without it I am as someone
lost from his caravan
a sandstorm whipping him;
someone out to find help on a frozen sea,
man alone on a waste of ice
imagining as the vast and hazy
emptiness, absorbs him
a tattered though victorious
humanity coming toward him,
soldiers linking arms,
a populace with banners
singing and beating drums.

Without it
I am cut off.
I await its sound.
I ravage memory
for sight of it, its melody.
I shape with bare
and desperate hands
its likeness in myself.

# The Calm

1.

Attempt at all times closeness to
the conflict you are in.
Not so as to dwell upon
dulling details of the cause
but to be aware of this:
that you are always in between
a white-clad calm that
at long intervals comes down
and the steady turmoil at the base:
a sea seething
a field devastated,
a man weeping, stone and dust
turned human for as long as
being human can be endured.

2.

Closeness to the conflict is
your nearness to its source.
The more fully a singer sings of
the pure anguish of your state,
the deeper the thought in you
that you too are being heard.
The turmoil in the water is often in
the surface that is thin.
When you cry because where you had been
the coast was calm, your small boat
in the sand left upside down,
the white-clad figure moving toward you
spanning sea and sun,
bemoan, bemoan it is no longer so!
The calm that will come again
                was long ago!

# Reply to a Friend in New England

I have your note.
Sorry to read you're lonely.
You have not found the joy you went for.
I know the bay you're visiting.
There the visual things
suggest the condition you feel,
flap in one's soul
like laundry hung to dry.
The sky is static there,
thin clouds the color of
swans' wings let through
a light that reaches corners
but has not the power
to illuminate.

Water beats against the stones
below the strip where people sit,
the boats out in the bay
look as though they give themselves
to being tossed about,
and not much happens.
The shadow of a bird
(wings spread fully out
the bird seems not to move,
seems painted on the air)
hovers over the reflection in
the water of a boat,
gray spreading over gray.
Shadows in this bay

that seek each other out,
cannot be kept apart,
nor does one blank the other out
escaping thus the separateness
that all decry, the flow
and sway of each with which
each must identify.
Is this then the law
that all must learn to live
who visit where you are
or any other strip of coast:
identity must be retained?
loneliness is part
of being self-contained?

In this bay where you have come,
where the coast is defined
by what you see —
by monotone and static sky —
you like others must confront:
the limited return
of what you want.
All day long the light is faint.
The repeated view of sails,
taken for white flags
implying hope, is bleak.
You have not found another way,
no other way but inward for
the self-assuring joy you seek.

# Shadowplay

Dead to the world, I was cast back
to move again among familiar shapes.
The state where I had been
cannot be described. There were
no objects there, but in
full strength and in pure form
the presence that takes speech
and mind away when feelings
are stirred by a person's momentary stay
pale as early evening in the door.

I knew when I was back it was
not nothingness had held me there.
That part in me which bears
no semblance to my body's line
on paper or in falling light
was then about to be received
like a cloth brought to be laid
across arms wide as space,
by a love gentler than air
and voices, voices behind clouds.

Not yet allowed, some forces dark
and fleeting came and drew me back—
from high walks where structures hold
all time and things that pass—
back to shadows that glide across
the shadow of my hands,
back to the movement of clouds,
the light at dark, the noted hush,
the moment of the figure in the door,
back to my repeated effort among
the things where I have walked before.

# Don Carlos, Saturday Afternoon

Alone! Who does not know the meaning of
alone? Granted, there is a world outside,
houses and streets are wet,
people run in and out of cars.
In the story sung on the air
each character is in the end alone.
A Spanish prince still loves the woman
who has become his father's bride.
A conquering Court attends the saving
of fallen Christians at the stake.
Although one hears a lofty gloria,
the prince in prison chains cries out,
betrayed, he thinks, by the one he loved
and by the friend in whom he believed.

Does it really help that being alone
in one condition shared by all?
The drama off-stage is no less complex.
Although one may assume that
disparate parts that do not always lock
in place are woven by a common thread,
the burden is not lessened for all that.
Not lessened by bewildered heads
and muffled cries, nor by the fact
that the sky's been agitated all day long,
that men in raincoats stumble across
slippery roofs, and that the very air
is dense with wriggling bacteria
which show up under a powerful glass.

# Exiled

Where will you go? Where now the rooms
once kept ready for you? the old
couple on hand to welcome you,
the garden just as it was when last
you visited, just as it was
as far back as you remember it—
golden the landscape when you stood there
late in the afternoon.

Where is it now, that place where you
belonged so naturally? the formal
growths, the house, the sunset-sights,
the dark turns of corridors—all these
as much alive in you then as they
were real then, summer after summer
in the country not far from town.
Now they are gone. Thoughts of them

stay on like tatters of a sail.
Memory will pale, and you have no
way now to turn and walk into
the interior you knew so well.
Another storm, one final gust,
your tattered thoughts will be as dust.
To keep alive the glow within
of what was once your ground, your home,
you need the plot, the trees, the stone.

# Late Last Night

Late last night we drove through fog:
nothing but a vague onslaught at
the window: vapors, or was it breath?

the clouds of the earth coming at us
all along the road. In the watery
substance all turned the same:

lights around corners, dreams behind
rooms, the country wide as oceans,
the singleness in every name.

# Irreconcilables

How to explain that on the day
we knew disease had invaded her
who had brought us into the world,
that death had conquered her like a weapon
she would not escape for long,
the winter sun spread vastly
and with utter ease
giving sharpness to each thing,
making all things stand out
as usually they don't:
a line of ships rooted like rocks,
and people in the frozen streets
free and light as the breath
that clung to them like clouds.

Along the edge of the cold sky
a strip of deep lavender ran
like a streamer in a wind
pulled by an invisible string,

and the water in the port
made over by days of cold
looked chopped but permanent, as if
the sea were chunks of bottleglass.

And everywhere surfaces
giving off the winter sun
in a sort of game of catch,
throwing at each the light
that each received, so that
the effect was a jubilation,
a juggler's feat so fast,
so intricate a trick, the full
extent of its multifarious display
escaped our eyes. But the sense
that it was there, and that

it meant not to deceive
but to reveal a joy
did not elude us.

Yet we were driving to get to her
who we feared might soon be gone.
And how were we to reconcile
exuberance with what we were about?

That a car was taking us
to the condition we call death,
that extinction could occur
when the day showed itself
in a display so bright
it seemed a game of light,
that disappearance should
make sense when all about us
objects we could not name
flared up in a cold winter sun
and shone until we had to turn
from them as from a flame,
nothing in us could reconcile,
nothing in us could explain.

# Gentle Lamb

At a street corner
waiting to cross: two boys.
Pressed against the chest of one
a dog slender as a greyhound,
timid as a lamb.

Traffic is heavy,
the boys are waiting for
a path to form.
Here in midtown New York
on a gray winter day,

they are a vision dimmed
in most, are the dream
flowing through their eyes and skin—
fire on this frost-
and world-encrusted ground.

And like a flare
sustained and surrounded by air,
the dog enfolded by
the boy's arm
rests on a tenderness

the boy is himself
seeking to express,
a tenderness before which he—
also at home in
an invisible mantle

that clings to him,
gentle as a lamb—
is himself dumb
as the animal
he carries in his arm.

# The Unworldliness That He Creates

1.

Alien in environments he has come to for the first time,
he is nevertheless at home in the eyes of those who look
upon the strangeness he creates,

is at home on streetcorners he chances on
where men stand about discussing events of which he
knows nothing,

is at home along the boulevards where the big hotels are,

in the parks at night when the crowds have left,

in the garden where on Sunday mornings there is music
of swans,
of peasant maidens lost to madness out of love,

is at home in these as a bird is above hillsides and towns
touched on for the first time.

2.

As a face becomes real when contained in a surface that
reflects,
as the soul has a inkling of what it can be
when received in the eyes of a stranger,

what among the things that depend upon
reception by the heart
is comparable to the recognition that

the flutter of wild ducks, the cry
of wild ducks whose object of pursuit
the observer cannot trace—only the cry

pierces the park as if despair
had been sounded on a trumpet—

that such happenings one mild afternoon
in a garden of a major capital,

that the aloofness of a swan, its utter lack of agitation,

that these suggest the cold majesty, the grave
beauty of total self-concern?

That these cries, these calls, these cruel attitudes and
gestures,

that the young man lying in the grass his face resting in
one hand,

that the old woman sitting under a dark tree,

that both, and countless more
letting what goes on around them go by them as if
the cry of ducks, the target lost behind shadows,
the poise of the swan, and the anguish,
the reception in the stranger's heart

were no more than a slight wind touching the leaves,
no more than clouds drifting by,
no more than the mild shadow of clouds...

To recognize that these are no more than a slight wind
touching the leaves;

to recognize that to experience these,
to let them be like a final phrase—
name, place, days, years chiseled roughly in rough stone—

to let them be part of the heart's reception means

they have achieved themselves

and having achieved themselves have become less than
formless

a thing for which there is no word
for it has not the shape of nothing

and received rests there as that,
as that without change....

3.

Who is he upon whom those who see him as a stranger
look as one looks upon someone who suggests a world at
once foreign and intimate, a world that though distant
reveals something one cannot quite visualize but has
yearned for, has said its name and responded with
tenderness...

who is he upon whom those who take him as a stranger
look and are amazed, for he recognizes himself in the
eyes of those he does not know, who all at once and for
a moment they cannot explain or even remember, know
him, and are astonished as they have been when absorbed
in the rarest of artworks, love words, songs of dreams...

who is he in whom the things he looks upon achieve
themselves?
He in whom their forms are released and become the
essence that he is, and is theirs?

Who is he who stands before a painting in which the
mother weeps, and the father weeps, and the son has
suffered all there is to be suffered?

Who is he who stands before this painting, and weeps?

4.

Whether he stands before a canvas whereon man's ultimate
condition is expressed through the most gentle, the most
beautiful body possible,

whether he sits on a bench on a Sunday
and receives in his eyes the light
and in his arms the flesh of the candles
the women that pass him have lit
out of love for their husbands
devotion to their children and duty to parents
in the churches they have left,

and receives as well the songs they intended
the ones joined in
and the ones that shook their bodies
as they knelt or stood against a pillar
and the thought of a loved one who had come and gone
bolted through them,

and receives also the looks and songs of the men
on the day away from their routine involvement.

On the horizon the boats they will not cease to construct.

Out of the waves, out of the sky
eyes into which they can continue to look

eyes that will return to them what they had wanted to
see

eyes that will make them what they had wanted to become

the look that will give them what they had or should
have had

the look that will wash away the darkness that had troubled
them

will lift them to their rightful place
and make them what they are.

They bow their heads,
in the evening pick up guitars for their songs of fate.

They weep over they know not what.
                                        Except that
though it may be nameless, it is closer to them
than the wind of the sea on their faces
and the light of midnight on their hair.

And infinite the shapes, the forms of tenderness
their yearning takes

*The expressed of the expression is always Love*
Love itself hath said

and the shapes that rise in their hearts and are dimmed
                                        in their eyes
are all as gentle, as beautiful as that body of love
that died and dies for love...

And receives this, the possibilities inside them,
their mostly unexpressed intention, the quality
that pours from them as though their bodies were a
                                        watery cloth
wrapped loosely around the quickest, brightest light,

as they stroll by him,
point a hand in his direction though they may be engaged
                                        in
conversation or may sit around a sidewalk table discussing
events of which he knows nothing

although at times they may look at him directly

and he is not there

198

only the look they seek
the eyes they know
the worship that is theirs:

the sign in the sky
the sails they construct.

5.

He in whom the pain in extremity is received and released

who is outside extremity or its pain could not be endured

he is not man, not woman,
he is not this, not that,
not I, not he, not you.

Movement transformed into art is an attempt to show this:

that form is so multifaceted it cannot be solid.
That color can only suggest color
and that color, movement and light
can only approximate
the quality the eye cannot behold,
the ear not catch,
the hand not endure.

And he who becomes he in the eyes of others,
who is alien regardless of the intimacy with which he
                                                    receives
the streets he walks on for the first time,

he who is stranger to those who marvel at the foreign
                                                    way
in which he moves—his ease as though gliding—

is it any wonder that when he comes into a street

when he sits on a bench or stands before a painting,

when the sky trembles in his eyes,

that he weeps?
          For what is he but response?

And he flows into that which flows into him as a wave
                                    into the sea

and the sea into waves
and both are water
both are one.

6.

Festive the crowds the evening before a day of
celebration in the square that was once first in the city
and is now famed for its age, style, agreeable proportions,
and the equestrian statue of a king in its center.

Tomorrow, they will go to the pools, will sing on the
roads, will lie on slopes, will eat on terraces overlooking
gorges, rivers, celebrated bridges, aqueducts, historic
sites; in the evening will follow suggestions of love
through crowded streets and squares with tall fountains
whose faint spray the air carries.

They have draped flags around the balconies, there are
candles on all tables of the restaurant fenced in by
boxed hedges, and many the languages among the people
who dine; those who are local stroll in groups under the
arcades, and the places where people eat and drink
standing up are crowded.

Is it because it is nevertheless the time when separateness
comes into its own, distinct as a shadow in front or
beside one, that he turns from these, runs from waiters,
from the sounds of food being served, from drifts of
conversations?

Is it because it is the time when those to whom streets and squares and the names of the flowers that look odd in the night along the coast are known in a language he cannot speak, are strangers as he is, the night before a celebration, each alone in the darkness?

In the taxi, back to the part of the city where the hotels
                                                    are

and elsewhere and later
down the broad road that runs along the coast
he does not resist it, lets it possess him:

the demands of the night in a land that is alien —

and walks into the air to be near the fountains
and feels on his hands and face the spray that the air
                                                    carries

and elsewhere and later
takes into himself all that the light of the moon on a
                        restless sea is suggestive of...

7.

When it is time to leave,
though he was alien where he has been,
and to those in whose language he cannot answer,
and to those who do not feel in him the possibilities in
                                                    man
and the background he reflects, is alien still:

he knows that he has been at home.

In paintings, the folds of rich garments, the dove that
                                        hovered,
the movement of figures upward, spearlike, flamelike as a
                                        prayer;

in the eyes of those who passed by him, sat near him,
who said much of themselves though not a word was said:

firm glimmers, kindling suggestions of what he knows best
rose to his demands and needs as waves to stormy wind.

As if on a stool near the chair of one through whom
birds roar, flowers sway, generations sing a tale—
from whom silence rises like a sword in flames—
attentive to murmurs that follow once the word was said
(what child has not experienced this?)

he knows he will be what those around him are

who will be what he is

and that they live not only in their songs and dreams
but also in the things they make—
things that retain their human presence like a hush—
and when he leaves
                    receives their looks
their flames in paintings
not as farewell
but beckoning, acknowledging wave . . .

and where he sat and walked

wherever there were those who looked upon the
            unworldliness that he creates

all that is air remembers him.

*Madrid, Lisbon, Cascais*

# Unalterables

Mistakes are dredged up again,
not mine but before mine began,
of figures I never knew,
and those I did know gone,
except that since what had
been done to them is carried on
through me, they lurk about,
unwelcome presences unseen
but evident like something

moving beneath dead leaves.
I thought I was done with them.
What need had I of faceless creatures,
agitation in their hair,
uttering unalterables
in languages I refused to hear?
Other sayings filled my ears,
other directions shook me — signs
that led to gates and guards who kept

the doom-promoters out. I realized
when I returned that doom or past
were unthinkable behind those gates,
but learned that they come back,
figures of my old mistakes,
who in spite of where I have been,
what I have found and seen,
want me to dance with them
their old, disordered dance.

# The Statue

For years I've tried to destroy
the statue in myself: baroque
facades I stood in front of
as a boy, strict rows of trees,
columns, fountains, pavilions,
sights meant for royal ease.

For harmony's sake I've tried
to rid myself of rigid
aspects. It's just as well
I don't succeed!
Someone departs, someone is wounded.
A woman runs across a street

her hands lifted in lament,
a grieving man walks from
a house with lowered head.
At moments such as these,
when pain runs through the body
and tensions flicker in a nervous sky,

the statue in a shadowed lane—
like a figure when a storm is gone—
breaks through in me, comes forth again:
and I observe with stone-
like eye, the dying
of what is meant to die.

# Two Poems on the Firebird

I—*Gift of the Firebird*

I will give you what you need.
Though I tremble, I am not weak.
What causes me to flutter
does not end. Free is what I am,
and you must let me free.
Who am I? The fire of my feathers,
my flaming presence only tells in part.
No one beholds all of what I am.
I may be in your eye and heart
but I am never owned.
No arms enfold me for long.
I yield so you will let me go.
Know though that my appearance here
in the shadow of golden fruit
shall not be in vain. My gift,
this fiery feather will remind you
you have held what you shall miss:
it will slay falsehoods and mists,
will free you from the grip of those
whose trickery does not live
unless you take it to be true.

## II—*Addressed to the Firebird*

Ever since I held you in my arms
(a flaming presence as I knew afterward)
what is unclear and ill-intended,
the murky force that thrives on refuse,
has been dispelled. All is now in place,
pale in pure light, each rising to its
full height and worth. All I
have done has flourished into fame:
but what is order, what is gain to me
who am bound to you, my bird of fire?

As time is piled on me like frost on leaves,
wherever I go, whatever I look at
it is our meeting I relive as in a haze:
I am young, you are under a tree
of golden fruit; I have stumbled on
your garden by mistake, or so I think;
I catch you, hold you; clasped in a dance
I demand, you yield; I entreat, you elude
being both coldness of a swan
and passion of a bird aflame;
too much nearness and, my senses lost,

I let you go. Since then your gift—
this fiery feather I am left with,
your promise in my mind and heart—
has brought health where withering was,
success in skills I wanted most.
But what is order, what is gain to me,
bound to you in no more than memory?
To have held you once should be enough,
but it is not: consumed by your flame—
a yearning beyond any worldly desire—
consuming me too slowly, too slowly,
my cruel bird of fire!

# History

What do we know of what is behind us?
The old town we drove through yesterday
is as remote from us now
as the century it was built,
water covering all our yesterdays equally.

What do we know of what lies ahead?
We see the old inns coming toward us,
white irregular walls, windows spaced unevenly,
women and children waiting at corners to cross.
We see the end of a town and the fields and forests beyond it,
but also hear the water waiting to cover them as we pass.

And what do we know
of what we do not see,
of what neither moves toward us
nor falls into watery wastes as we pass?

# Old Coat

Years have gone by, forty and some,
and I am suddenly aware
they have. The pangs, the feeling
that the marvelous exists somewhere,
is about to begin when I have looked in a face
and have found there submerged
one of many dreams; the feeling
that what I really am is in
the yearning most men are not conscious of—
for that horse in gilded cloth
trotting with lowered mane
toward that bright tower out of sight—
all of that, all of that is just the same.

I see an Emperor on stage.
He is dressed in the blue of skies,
a stiff glove is on one hand,
bow and arrow in the one that's bare.
*Falcon*, it seems to me he cries,
*Falcon, you led me to my fondest wish.*
*Withered is all, ash my hunt*
*now your red wing is gone!*
*Falcon, my falcon, return!*
Away from him I am
his language hard to discern,
the torment in his face,
the agony of his distress.
None of this has changed.
But years have gone.
I have sat in rooms
ablaze, way out, and out of sight.
I returned dragging an old coat behind,

black blotch on the floor,
painful old shadow
dark as blindness and failure,
a coat handed down, a coat
I have not the strength to throw away:
mantle that in the end is all
the gorgeously attired fighter has
to protect him in battle
and cover his death. Years
have not dissolved this ancient shield, this skin—
though it wears out in spots
I am obliged to mend, or have it done.
                              Old women
chant on      chant on
as practiced fingers sew.

# The Tenuous Line

Listen now, listen to this:
the line you must hold on to
is tenuous, but it is all
you have to help you on.
You cannot for a moment forget
where you have been,
and what and where it is
you must clear the way
to reach.

You are not Theseus
but you too must have combat with
shapes half human and half beast.
All your desires must be faced,
and your desire for
the beautiful—to dally,
be entangled with
the deeply sensual—
leads you to this.

Unlike Ariadne I take
no girlish interest in you.
But to get to where you are going
you must defeat
what breaks out on the way.
And this you cannot do
without impersonal aid.
My voice you must learn
to listen to,

the tenuous line, to see.
The curious fact of this
your labyrinthian path is:
there is not one desire,
not one nagging call

210

that lingers in your dreams
that you shall miss.
What you have asked for
you shall have: triumphal

visits with cities of
the past; intercourse
on flowerbeds with
beauties of the night;
tears on sensitive faces
in response to
what you are, what you,
by saying, by a
lament, a smile, have hinted at.

You will not be denied any
of this, but this:
what you hold you will not keep.
Applause you will not assume
as yours. Like this thread
you will not be attached
to any of what
lies on your path—
*unless, of course, unless...*

Your gain will be in other ways.
Besieged, you will not shun
the hateful looks, the trumpet
blares, the outraged cries.
At dawn, you will hold
perfection on your eyes.
You will not say: "I've had
enough, have had my fill!"
but will ask to move on, move on—
*until, of course, until...*

# The Look Back

From you
I ask this simple act:
look back at me as if
recollecting your whole life
and most of all
your deepest wants.
Look back at me in a way
that will let me look at you
as if in our eyes
fortifications dissolved to dust
and dust into space. Look at me

as if to say, Now I have
looked into myself.
Symbols of timelessness,
stone trimmings, stone heads and stares,
powerful embodiments, drift there
as in watery surfaces—
lamplights that lead us back
into a past that is.
Only by feeling close to that
which we can never reach
but lasts are we
enlarged and comforted.

# Les Nuits d'Eté

The soul yearns for trees
rustling on summer nights,
for bays where are reflected
windows, faces that hesitate
to do more than suggest
feelings that brought them to the ledge.

The soul yearns for recognition.
To declare what cannot be said
is not its agitation.
To be received, to let its wings
be felt like a bird in its
ample cage where beautifully,

sorrowfully it sings.
To be denied its own reflection
is the soul's relentless grief.
Not to be acknowledged,
not understood — be it
in towns, by the sea,
in shimmering woods.

# Process of Recapturing

There, in the dim room
where bodies move across
like tall shadows on walls,
nothing will be given back to you,
nothing of what was not, be found.

Even those days years back
when you searched for the friend
to recapture for each the past,
even when what was lost,
when the love that should have been
seemed near at hand, among

young bathers on the lawns,
in tree-lined streets deserted when
the late spring sun went down:
much less of what you thought
could happen, happened even then.

Loss, pain of the parent
always close, absence of
the one you needed most,
you have sought in
body engagement to express
and find in body forgetfulness.

Have soothed the body in your arms,
have loved as though you held
the love you were denied,
have wakened when the other left,
have wakened when the other cried.

The process of recapturing
is both this letdown and
this gain: you learn
what cannot be again, but that
the essence of what was—
if not its form—is in what is.


# On Behalf of Orpheus

Furies, let the singer pass!
Clear the track,
tear aside the languorous shades,
the long cobwebs
that kill the way.
He who must sing
must cross all this.

The lusts and self-
indulgences you are
do not incite him much
and he need not pursue,
sees only darkness where
you howl and thrive:
dissolve, and let him through!

He is strumming a lament
for you, is ready to live
in ceaseless strain
to reach perfection in
his art, also your song—
but can do so only in
the neighboring world
where you do not belong!

# Wind to Human Voice

Remember, my elusiveness
remains. All flows, all I
bring with me goes. Is it not
enough it stays, the touch
that tears across your face?
*No*   you whisper   *no*

To suffer that all passes
is as natural for you
as tearing past is true for me.
By your pain do I learn what I am.
But you too could learn that this,
my freedom, is your own.

Your face shows torment at
each loss. Can you not also see
the endless stream I bring
of light, of shade, and air?
Can you not be content with
this unfailing interplay

of sun on summer grass,
of frost on foliage,
of lamps in chilly rooms?
Must you persist, must you
bemoan each time
when you are weary that

those days years back
when you ran from the sand
up to the terrace of
the summer house where you
were called, will not return?
Can you not remember instead

that you are here, although
that boy you were is dead?
That the light where waves
break out of sight
still glimmers in your head?
That in the waters' depth

the sheen is undisturbed,
only the surfaces are rough
and foul with glare? Can you
not find some comfort in
the changeless nature of my ways?
*Not enough*  you whisper  *not enough*

# Wilderness Child

1.

Nature was his bread,
water he loved.
The moon shimmered in the stream
he put his hands into to drink.
The moon fell through the trees
when he looked up.
Night was a silvery web.
His world of foliage and sky
trembled like a spider's threads
beneath his hands and legs.
All by himself, he howled,
not knowing how to be secure,
not knowing why the sky drifts past,
not knowing why.

2.

The hand of the man
was closer than the moon.
He took it and placed it on his head.
He pressed his cheek to the woman's breast.
What they meant and what he was
was in their eyes, their hands, and his.
His world in the wilderness
had passed him like a cloud—
not this. Here he has found
the touch and nearness with him
when he sleeps and wakes.

3.

He stands by the open window
and looks across the meadow
toward the dark wood. He has a bowl
of water in his hands. He weeps.
Is this the first time he is feeling sad?
He cannot speak but like
an animal cries out. For what
he lost? found? For what he never had?

# Like Laocoön

Like Laocoön
in the power of
a will
an order
men must act out
be it to their detriment
a will that works
its rule through them
a will they can
enact but not control

Like Laocoön
serpents wrapped around
his shoulders and
his legs
thick slippery ropes
a pull as of the sea
dragging to take him
into their own
turmoil and lair
the exact opposite of where
he may have striven
all his years to get

Like Laocoön
his head
his shoulders turned from
the slime sent
to bring him down
so that the other side
favored by *this* god
may win

Like Laocoön
his gaze fixed on
his besieged town
his mind looking beyond
to the calm
the spacious pavilions
the defenders
may think about
but cannot now see

—the high uplands
their zone
of safety
everyman's
promised return—

so do I—
like Laocoön held
by unremitting pulls—
turn toward You
Immutable
Spine   Column
Invisible
Center that
can never fall apart

and plead
to endure

# About the Author

ARTHUR GREGOR came to the United States from his native Vienna during World War II, at the age of fifteen, and has since lived in New York City, except for periods of travel and a year in northern California when he taught at the California State University at Hayward. In 1948, *Poetry* awarded him its First Appearance Prize, and he has since contributed regularly to the major journals including *Southern Review, Sewanee Review, Kenyon Review, Hudson Review, Poetry, The Nation, The New Yorker, Harper's Magazine* and many others. *Embodiment* And Other Poems is his eighth collection of poems, which include *Figure in the Door* (1968), *A Bed by the Sea* (1970), *Selected Poems* (1971), and *The Past Now* (1975). He has also written books for children and has had three plays produced. After a career in magazine and book publishing, Arthur Gregor is now Professor of English at Hofstra University where he also directs its Creative Writing and Publishing Studies Programs.